THE CRISIS OF THE
REFORMATION

NORMAN SYKES, Dean of Winchester from 1958 until his death in 1961, was born in 1897 in Liversedge, Yorkshire. He was educated at Leeds University and Queen's College, Oxford, where he took his D. Phil. in 1923. From 1924 to 1931 he lectured in history at King's College, University of London. He then became Professor of History, University College of the South-West, Exeter (1931-33); Birkbeck Lecturer in Ecclesiastical History, Trinity College, Cambridge (1931-33); and Dixie Professor of Ecclesiastical History, Trinity College, Cambridge (1944-58). He was an Honorary Fellow of Emmanuel College, Cambridge. His many books include: *Church and State in England since the Reformation* (1929); *Church and State in England in the Eighteenth Century* (1934); *The Crisis of the Reformation* (1938); *The English Religious Traditions* (1953); and *Old Priest and New Presbyter* (1956).

MEDIEVAL AND EARLY MODERN EUROPEAN HISTORY TITLES IN NORTON PAPERBACK EDITIONS

THE CRISIS OF THE
REFORMATION

By

NORMAN SYKES

W · W · NORTON & COMPANY · INC ·
NEW YORK

Books That Live
The Norton imprint on a book means that in the publisher's
estimation it is a book not for a single season but for the years.
W. W. Norton & Company, Inc.

PRINTED IN THE UNITED STATES OF AMERICA

1 2 3 4 5 6 7 8 9 0

To
MY WIFE

PREFACE

THIS little book, composed originally in 1938 for delivery in fulfilment of my duties as canon theologian of Liverpool Cathedral, and published in the year commemorating the quater-centenary of the English Bible, suffered the fate of many worthier compilations in being consumed by fire from heaven during the war. When the Centenary Press decided to reissue it, I had to decide whether I ought completely to rewrite it, or to allow its reissue in its original form. Nobody is more quickly or completely aware of the defects of a volume than its author; and no student of history could have lived through the years of war without learning something more of the subject of this little study. My first desire was to rewrite it entirely; but it seemed on second thoughts better to allow its reprinting without substantial alteration. I have made therefore only a few corrections of fact. For the rest I can only say what I said in my preface to the original version in 1938, that the volume makes no claim either to originality or completeness. It offers an interpretation which it is hoped may not be without stimulus, if only to refutation, to other students of Church history whose interest draws them the like way.

EMMANUEL COLLEGE, CAMBRIDGE,
1946.

CONTENTS

CHAPTER I

THE CAUSES OF THE REFORMATION

" IF the methods of 1688 produce no result, corruption of the body politic demands a 1789." The words of Dr. Figgis have a particular relevance to the Reformation movement of the sixteenth century. It sprang fundamentally from recognition of the urgent necessity for reform of the Church in head and members, and its outward circumstances were determined by the failure of previous attempts to effect reformation through the existing constitutional organs of the Church. The need for thoroughgoing reform indeed had been long and universally admitted, and was ultimately attained, within countries remaining faithful to the papal allegiance, through the agency of the Council of Trent. But the failure of the methods of 1688 had meanwhile provoked the employment of the more violent measures of 1789 in other countries, and reform had been translated into repudiation of the authority of the Apostolic See, so that the efforts of the Tridentine fathers came too late to recover all the lost ground. The Reformation movement in its early stages fell upon an unprepared and unreformed Papacy with the force of an avalanche, appearing at first almost irresistible. Nor can its importance be minimised by criticism of the character of Luther or of Henry VIII, nor by facile phrases which account it to have been ' made in Germany '. It is essential for fruitful discussion of the Reformation to bear in mind the difference between occasion and cause. In many cases the occasion may seem trivial or even discreditable; but the very insufficiency of such merely personal episodes as the ' divorce ' of Henry VIII or the polemic of Luther against indulgences to sustain the weight of the ensuing religious revolution is a warning to the student to look more deeply. Fundamentally the Reformation was a revolution and it was concerned ultimately with the deepest elements in religion.

This does not exclude the part played in the fashioning of its course by a variety of other factors not primarily religious in character. The Reformation was affected profoundly by a diversity of circumstances, political, economic, geographical, and philosophical; and in some cases one or more of these elements may seem to have exercised a predominating influence over the religious and theological elements. Whilst giving due place to each of these secular considerations, however, care must be taken not to lose sight of what underlay the movement viewed as a whole, namely the grave issues of faith and practice controverted and discussed throughout Europe.

The existence of administrative and financial abuses in the Church, and especially in the papal Curia, was widely recognised in the fifteenth century. Political and financial exigencies had compelled the Papacy to devote an increasing attention to its situation as one of the many contending civil states in the Italian peninsula, diminishing thereby its spiritual authority. Temporal kings and princes accustomed to regard the Papacy on its political side as a piece in the diplomatic and military game of a balance of power were little disposed to pay regard to its ecclesiastical censures, which were in fact often inextricably entangled with its secular policy. If the Emperor Charles V found Pope Clement VII complaisant owing to political difficulties, far otherwise was his experience of Paul IV, whose hostility to the influence of Spanish power in Italy led to his declaration of war against Philip II of Spain in 1556. The protracted episodes of the Avignon Papacy and the Great Schism had tended insensibly to detract from the religious authority of the Apostolic See; and, even more important in practical consequence, had led to a great extension of the financial exactions of the Curia. The Avignon Papacy had perfected a system of financial centralisation which its successors had gratefully continued; and which, though necessary to the political situation of the Papacy in Italy, to its judicial and administrative direction of the whole Church, and to its ambition to become a munificent patron of the Renaissance arts and letters, imposed burdens too heavy to be borne upon the several national kingdoms. The multiplication of papal claims to provision provoked reprisals from secular rulers, whilst the

Papacy itself became dependent in practice upon the banking houses of the fifteenth century, whose co-operation was necessary not only in advancing loans to the popes but in collecting its internationally-derived revenue. The Avignon Papacy set the pattern for its successors by its patronage of the arts, which increased its financial responsibilities; and with the influence of Renaissance standards in letters there came also an evil infiltration in the sphere of morals. It is not necessary to enter into details of, or to lay undue emphasis upon, the personal lives of some of the Renaissance popes, save as a warning against similar emphasis on the personal morality of Henry VIII or Luther. More important was the general tendency to regard the Papacy as simply one political state amongst others and to confront its claims to a universal spiritual authority with practical evidences of papal policy in the spheres of diplomacy and finance.

Reform was needed not only in the head, but throughout the members, of the Church. Not only at Rome but in all the kingdoms of Western Christendom did the world seem to have gained a victory over the Church. In England, the diocesan episcopate during the reign of Henry VII and the early years of Henry VIII was characterised by its lack of theologians and by its absorption in secular affairs. Such prelates as Robert Sherburne, of St. David's (to which see he forged a papal bull in his own favour) and Chichester, and Richard Fox, of Exeter, Bath and Wells, Durham, and Winchester, were typical of an episcopate largely recruited from the clerks of the royal household; for Fox was so occupied as a diplomatist and statesman that he never saw his cathedrals at Exeter and Wells, and only during the last six years of his life devoted himself to the ecclesiastical duties of his office. At the summit of worldliness stood Wolsey himself, holding *in commendam* with the Archbishopric of York the sees of Durham and Winchester in succession, in addition to his pensions from the sees of Tournai in France and Badajoz in Spain, and the abbacy of St. Albans. Illuminating evidence of the impact of papal diplomacy upon the Church was furnished by the fact that the see of Worcester for forty years before the Reformation was occupied by a series of Italian prelates, immersed in the necessary negotiations between England and the

Curia, whilst two other Italians, Adrian de Castello and Lorenzo Campeggio, also held English bishoprics.

Similar conditions prevailed in the Gallican Church, where Cardinal d'Estouteville rivalled the English Wolsey in pluralism, since, although living in Italy and holding a bishopric there, he possessed in France one archbishopric, three bishoprics, four abbeys, and three priories. Cardinal Jean de Lorraine was appointed coadjutor of Metz at the tender age of three ; whilst the more famous Cardinal of that name, Charles de Guise (himself a notable reforming prelate) received the archbishopric of Reims at the age of fourteen, though he was not consecrated to the episcopate till the age of twenty in 1545. Upon the death of his uncle Jean, Charles in 1551 became Bishop of Metz, administrator of the temporalties of the see of Verdun, abbot *in commendam* of ten abbeys, and first Cardinal of Lorraine. Abbacies indeed seemed to exist for the purpose of being held *in commendam*. In Germany the episcopate was commonly treated as a provision for princely families, pluralities were common, and consecration or even ordination to the priesthood was long postponed by some bishops-elect. The career of Albert of Brandenburg was typical of the state of the German episcopate. Nor were the inferior clergy slow to follow such examples where opportunity offered, as in the cathedral and collegiate churches with their great number of benefices *sine cura animarum*, which presented, like abbeys, a happy hunting-ground for clerical careerists; for some cathedrals, as Lincoln and Salisbury in England, had between fifty and sixty prebends, the duties of which were nominal. Throughout the ecclesiastical organisation there was abundant need for reform; though it should not be supposed that either the Reformation or the Counter-Reformation succeeded entirely in removing the abuses of pluralism. In England the extent of pluralism was restricted, but the practice itself continued to be exploited and abused until the beginning of the reign of Victoria; whilst in France the unreformed system continued with little amelioration until the Revolution of 1789.

The religious Orders did not escape the prevalent worldliness and laxity, but stood likewise in urgent need of reformation. The vocation to the life of religion was undoubtedly a declining

influence during the fourteenth and fifteenth centuries, and this
fall in numbers affected seriously the position and strength of
the several houses. Indeed, the general impression produced in
regard to the religious Orders is one of financial difficulties,
dwindling personnel, and spreading laxity. In many cases monasteries were burdened by corrodies and pensions; in others their
inefficient administration of property and estates was productive
of further insolvency, whilst the value of their social services in
education and hospitality was decreasing in varying degrees.
Nor had the Friars avoided the corruption which naturally
followed the corporate acquisition of wealth and property.
From the standpoint of religion it is difficult to escape the persuasion that the religious Orders could not justify their position
in view of the widespread decay of zeal and intrusion of laxity;
and in view of changing economic conditions and the rise of the
middle classes some measures of disendowment of monastic
houses seemed probable and bearing the promise of benefit to
the community.

Such abuses in administration might, however, be remedied
if a vigorous and reforming pope could secure election to the
chair of St. Peter. It was the grave responsibility of the Papacy
that the urgent necessity for reform was not realised until so
great a part of Christian Europe had repudiated its allegiance.
If the Church were to be reformed from within and by the
restoration of its own machinery, the zeal and determination of
a Hildebrand would be required. Indeed, the most hopeful line
of reform might have seemed to be the recurrence of such an
episcopal revival as had prepared the way for the pontificate of
Gregory VII. It was the misfortune of the Church that the
endeavours towards a restoration of episcopal action and independence which the Conciliar movement had promised to in-
augurate, had failed to produce the desired end. To the theorists
and practical champions of the Conciliar movement, a programme of reform of the Church in head and members which
would decentralise the ecclesiastical administration and give back
much of the initiative which the episcopate had lost, had given
much hope of success. The collapse of this experiment in constitutional readjustment had left the Papacy master of the situa-

tion; and the several concordats which were made with the
rulers of the rising national states were of little service to the
cause of reform. Rather they delivered the episcopate and the
churches to the rival pretensions of pope and king, each ruler
making the best bargain for himself and both joining to plunder
the ecclesiastical society.

In particular Papacy and monarchy divided the episcopal
nominations between their respective favourites; and no difficulty
was raised from Rome when, for example, kings and their prelates wished to suppress smaller religious houses and to divert
their revenues to other purposes. For the moment this division
of the spoil might content both parties, but in view of the
increasing secularisation of the Papacy and its absorption in
political intrigue and diplomacy in Italy, the moment might
soon come when the interests of pope and kings would clash.
In such an eventuality the national episcopate would certainly be
in no position to resist the will of the civil sovereign, and might
be moved by no sense of loyalty or gratitude towards the Roman
Papacy. If the king should resolve to reform the Church within
his kingdom, neither pope nor bishops would have the strength
to offer effective resistance. It was the peculiarity of the Spanish
reforming movement that it was carried through by the monarchy supported by Cardinal Ximenes against the wishes of the
Papacy, which was forced into reluctant acquiescence and acceptance of its results. Similarly it is impossible to study the English
Reformation without remarking the readiness of such orthodox
prelates as Gardiner and Tunstall to acquiesce in Henry VIII's
repudiation of papal supremacy, and even, in the case of the
former, to defend it in writing as well as by action. Such a standpoint is itself a measure of the decline of papal prestige even
within the Church.

Equally important, if not more influential in determining the
nature of the Reformation movement of the sixteenth century,
with the administrative abuses of the Church and the secularisation of the Papacy, were the intellectual and religious forces
tending towards the disintegration of the traditional order. So
far back as the first quarter of the fourteenth century Marsilius
of Padua in his *Defensor Pacis*, published in 1324, had set the

fashion of a new movement of thought upon the problems of political government. Written almost two centuries before the Reformation, it was not without significance that an English translation of this work was printed in 1535 for controversial purposes by William Marshall, who sought the patronage of Thomas Cromwell. The remedies prescribed by Marsilius for fourteenth-century Italy were relevant to the case of sixteenth-century Europe. For Marsilius, like Dante, stood unequivocally for the supremacy of the civil government against the Papacy. Indeed, he dealt drastically with the pretensions of the ecclesiastical society, holding that in matters spiritual the New Testament was the only authoritative law of God, from which the Papacy possessed no power of dispensation. Further, he argued that Scripture allows no authority to compel obedience even to the laws of the Gospel, so that the clergy were physicians of the soul only by the exercise of persuasion in teaching and warning. To Marsilius all faithful Christians were churchmen, *viri ecclesiastici*, and the only authority exercising a universal claim on Christians was a *Generale Concilium Fidelium*, including priests and laity as well as the episcopate. Although he allowed to the Church an organised ministry, he argued for the equality of all bishops, and denied to Rome any primacy beyond that of honour, as, for example, the professors at Orléans might defer to the judgment of the great doctors of Paris in academic matters. This radical criticism prepared the way for a thorough-going exaltation of the position and authority of the State, since with the ignoring of the papal supremacy there went the denial of the authority of the Canon Law. The State became the superior power, having at its disposal the revenues of ecclesiastical corporations, having the right to summon general councils and to confirm their decisions, and exercising no compulsion in matters of belief, but deciding according to its own free judgment what, if any, ecclesiastical censures should be supported by the coercive power of the civil arm. Dr. Previté-Orton, the latest editor of the *Defensor Pacis*, summarises the teaching of Marsilius as " an affection for his Presbyterian system, his Erastianism, and a passionate republicanism ... bred in an Italian commune, hating the ecclesiastical powers which put it out of gear, and anxious to combine the sharply bounded and compact unitary state which he loved with a kind of Society of Christendom guided by its elected advisory General Council ".

In other, and perhaps more vital, fields of intellectual activity the mental climate was favourable to change. Laurentius Valla and Nicholas of Cusa demonstrated the falsity of the Donation of Constantine and the Forged Isidorean Decretals, two of the chief proof-texts of papal supremacy; and the work thus begun in the field of history was carried backwards into that of the Bible itself. The work of Renaissance scholars towards the recovery of as good texts as possible of the Hebrew version of the Old Testament and the Greek of the New led to important results. For though the discovery of correct versions of the original languages of the Bible was in itself neutral, it helped to discredit the massive theological edifice which had been erected on the basis of the Vulgate. Many students participated in this labour, notably Johann Reuchlin, the Hebraist, but the most influential of all was the cosmopolitan scholar Erasmus, whose editions of the Greek New Testament and of the Greek patristic writings prepared the way for a new and critical attitude towards the papal system. In general, the study of the early history of the Christian Church in the apostolic and post-apostolic ages presented a picture of a pre-papal Christian organisation which stood in marked contrast with the claims of the Papacy to the status of University Ordinary. Hence conservative scholars of the eminence of Erasmus could join with moderate reformers of the calibre of Stephen Gardiner in doubting the necessity of the Papacy to the organisation of the Church. In other respects also the appeal to the Bible afforded arguments in favour of the civil power in its contest with Rome. The Old Testament was invaluable in its picture of the polity of the chosen people of the Old Covenant, in which kings as nursing fathers of the Jewish Church had exercised authority over the priesthood as well as the laity of the Hebrew nation. Not only Anglican apologists could make their appeal to this pattern in behalf of the Royal Supremacy, but Luther also in support of his enlistment of the help of the princes in Germany. It would be difficult to exaggerate the influence of Old Testament precedents for the ' godly prince' (typified by David, Solomon, Josiah, and Hezekiah) and their service to the reformers' cause.

Even more important was the widespread circulation of vernacular translations of the Bible, and their rapid multiplication as a consequence of the invention of printing. Henceforth instead of the few and laboriously produced copies of the vernacular Scriptures, large quantities were distributed for the edification of the people. The thrice-told tale of the revolution wrought in religious ideas by the translations which rendered 'presbuteros' and 'episkopos' not as 'sacerdos' or 'priest' and 'bishop' but as 'elder' and 'superintendent', which read 'ekklesia' not as 'ecclesia' or 'church' but as 'congregation', and 'metanoein' not as 'facere poenitentiam' or 'do penance' but as 'change one's attitude', is important as illustrating the far-reaching sanctions given to reform by such new conceptions. In such a mental atmosphere it was easy for zealous reformers to pass beyond the cautious indifference of Erasmus towards papal claims, to a demand for root and branch repudiation of all connection with the see of Rome. The cumulative effect of historical and Biblical studies pursued at first with the scholar's detachment was seen in the market-place, where restraint and moderation were virtues of less prize.

Within the more rarified atmosphere of the universities too the scholastic philosophy was a declining system, which in its decay provoked biting satire and ridicule. The creative epoch of the thirteenth century was long overpast; and since its close— for Duns Scotus himself died in 1307—scholasticism had reached the end of its constructive period. Henceforth its energies were spent in development, repetition, and refinement of former principles, which offered an easy target for the irony of its opponents. The *Via Nova*, as the School of Nominalism became known, held that reality inhered in particular things, not in general concepts, in contradiction to the Realists of the *Via Antiqua*, the tradition of St. Thomas. Not even a return to St. Thomas could avail the disciples of scholasticism; for so convinced a Realist as Wyclif had rejoiced to give reasons for a rejection of the doctrine of Transubstantiation upon grounds common to the schoolmen.

These tendencies however were operative mainly in the limited circles of educated society, which, despite the emergence of literate laymen, were small in number. Speculations concerning the relations of civil and spiritual authority, or even critical studies of historical and Biblical proof-texts, were not calculated to appeal to the generality of either the clergy or laity, who were too ignorant to understand their purport. If the movements towards reform had been restricted to the political ambitions of kings, or the predatory appetites of the middle classes for monastic estates, or the ridicule of scholars for the ignorance of the parish priests, the character of the Reformation would assuredly have been different. Beneath these high matters of State and churchcraft were popular religious tendencies and influences which played an important part alike in the preparation and fashioning of the sixteenth-century changes. At the heart of medieval catholicism lay the Mass. At this dramatic representation of the act of man's redemption every layman was expected to be present on Sundays and Holy Days; and once at least each year, at Eastertide, to receive the Holy Communion. During the later Middle Ages however the Mass became inextricably associated in the popular mind with many superstitious ideas. Particularly the fourteenth and fifteenth centuries witnessed a great growth of the practice of offering masses for the delivery of the souls of the departed from purgatory, which was reflected in the widespread endowment of chantries and the building of chantry chapels in cathedrals, abbeys, collegiate and parish churches.

> It was on this widespread belief in the quantitative, assignable, and so marketable value of each Mass, coupled with a belief in a penal Purgatory, that the popular religion of calculation and fear was based which characterised the later Middle Ages, and produced the endless multiplication of Masses. And this is the testimony of the Chantry system to the real meaning of the later medieval teaching about the Eucharistic Sacrifice. It was assumed that each Mass was in itself a distinct act of sacrifice; and that the more Masses the faithful got applied for them, the more fruit they obtained.

The conclusions of Dr. B. J. Kidd from his survey of the *Later Medieval Doctrine of the Eucharistic Sacrifice* are supported by those of Mr. B. L. Manning in his study of *The People's Faith in the Time of Wyclif.*

> The popular view of the Mass was distinctly mechanical. The tenor of wills and anecdotes shows unmistakably that the layman was taught to believe that he could increase the effect of Eucharistic prayers by the simple process of multiplying them or making them more elaborate. The benefits which the living and the dead received varied in direct proportion with the number and magnificence of the Masses said, and with the amount of offering made at each.

The extraordinary character of some of the provisions for requiem Masses finds illustration in wills of the period. Thus in England Henry V provided by will for the saying of 20,000 Masses for the repose of his soul, though it is doubtful if this large total was ever discharged; whilst the Earl of Oxford, who died in 1509, ordered 2000 Masses to be said for him in monastic houses of which he was founder. The wealthy Lord Mayor of London who was father to Dean Colet likewise provided by his will for two priests to say Mass daily for the space of fifteen years for his soul; and, most remarkable of all, perhaps, was the provision by the Lady Alice West who died in 1395 for the saying within a fortnight of her death of 4400 Masses, for which she bequeathed the sum of £18 10s., an instance of urgency combined with extreme parsimony, for the fee offered was only one penny a Mass. Such multiplication and arithmetical valuation of Masses led naturally to superstitious and degraded conceptions of its nature amongst the laity, and were the parents of a widespread popular repugnance to the Mass. Nothing could be more erroneous than to suppose that popular aversion to the Church was confined to financial, judicial, or administrative abuses, and did not extend to matters of belief and practice. The volume of tracts and broadsides directed against the corruptions and superstitious ideas associated with the Mass, which poured forth in Germany when Luther had opened the floodgates of criticism, or in England when Protector Somerset essayed his brief experiment in freedom of religious propaganda, or were typified by the Placards against the Mass in France, were evidence and fruit of a widespread popular revulsion. It would have been strange indeed if the Reformation movements had passed by the central rite of the Medieval Church. Rather they tended themselves to proceed by reaction to extremes (so that Calvin denounced the Mass as *summum illud abominationum omnium caput*), and to produce in some quarters a denial of any sacrificial character of the Eucharist. But it is impossible to avoid being impressed by evidences of the repugnance of the laity to such mechanical and arithmetical valuations of the Mass as were the result of the multiplication of obits. It was not without significance that the will of John Colet, dean of St. Paul's, contained no provision for Masses for the repose of his soul, nor aspirations for the suffrages of the Blessed Virgin Mary and the saints.

Furthermore, the abuses associated with the Mass led to a grave degradation of the office of the priesthood. Since one Mass was as good as another, whether said by an illiterate or learned, a devout or immoral, priest, the personal character and education of the priests became matters of comparative unimportance. But since only a person possessed of Priest's Orders could say Mass, with the multiplication of requiem Masses there came a natural demand for more priests to discharge the duty. Accordingly bishops, in defiance of the prohibition of Canon Law against ordaining persons without title or a sufficient income on which to maintain themselves, admitted to the priesthood large numbers of candidates, whose education was often limited to the ability to repeat the Latin of the Mass. Aspirants to the priesthood tramped from diocese to diocese in search of a bishop about to ordain, and after ordination tramped again seeking employment as Mass-priests. Their rate of remuneration was generally low, and their security of a livelihood precarious. The natural result of the growth of a class of Mass-priests of uncertain education and somewhat vagrant life was contempt of the order of Priesthood. One of the most striking consequences of this contempt was the disinclination of the more prosperous clergy to receive Priest's Orders; for in cathedrals which had undertaken the responsibility of obits chaplains could be hired to discharge the duty, whilst amongst the beneficed secular clergy the temptation was strong to hire a priest to perform the sacramental offices, thus allowing the rector or vicar to indulge a taste for non-residence. A remarkable survival of this disesteem of the priesthood and of the preference of cathedral dignitaries to remain in minor Orders was seen in England, where not until 1662 was the possession of Priest's Orders needful for admission to a cathedral prebend or residentiaryship. The result therefore of the degradation of the priesthood was a decline in standards of clerical education. When Bishop Hooper visited the English diocese of Gloucester in 1551 he found that out of a total of 311 clergy, 171 could not repeat the Ten Commandments, 33 could not say in what chapter they were to be found, 10 could not say the Lord's Prayer, 27 were ignorant who was its author, 30 could not say where it was to be found, and two ventured the affirmation that it was so-called because the Lord King had commanded its use.

Another notable characteristic of religion in the later Middle Ages was the popularity of sacred relics. Pre-eminent amongst devotees of this cult was Frederick the Wise, elector of Saxony, who became the patron of Luther, and who had amassed a vast collection of relics, procured from a great variety of markets. When in 1509 a catalogue of his collection was printed it was found that in the church which he had endowed at Wittenberg there were no fewer than 5005 such articles. The quantity and curious character of relics throughout Christendom were indeed remarkable. Miraculous images of the Blessed Virgin were numerous, for the epoch witnessed a great popular devotion to our Lady, testified by the spread of the Rosary and by such extravagances as her salutation as " the eternal daughter of the eternal Father, the heart of the indivisible Trinity " and even " Glory be to the Virgin, to the Father, and to the Son ". Devotion to the Virgin, however, was at least edifying, a quality which could hardly be affirmed of some aspects of the hunt for relics; as at Reading, which claimed to possess part of the rope with which Judas hanged himself. Other relics were believed most efficacious in filling the place which has been usurped in modern society by patent medicines and mascots. Thus a skull of Petronilla at Bury St. Edmund's cured fevers, and a bell of St. Guthlac at Repton priory healed diseases of the head. Associated with the respect for relics were pilgrimages to the shrines

at which the most famous saints of Christendom were com-
memorated. Compostella was third only to the tombs of the
Apostles at Rome and to the Holy Land as a place of efficacious
pilgrimage; and St. Thomas of Canterbury was especially
popular in England. When Erasmus and Colet paid a visit to
Canterbury in 1513 they found there an amazing collection of
relics, including St. Thomas's maniple with his perspiration and
blood still visible, and, in addition to the relics of the martyr
himself, a varied assortment of other ' skulls, jawbones, teeth,
hands, fingers, and whole arms '. The competition for the
possession of sacred objects spread to private individuals, whose
wealth and travels had enabled them to secure such treasures;
as Sir Thomas Cumberworth of Somerby, Lincolnshire, who
bequeathed by his will in 1451 to the chantry priests of Somerby
Church his " lityll cros of gold . . . with the peis of the peler
that oueere Lord was Skowrged upon yerin, a pais of the
Roche yat ouere lady mylk es in & the ele of Saynt kateryn
and of sant hoght in glasie ". Amidst such by-ways of devotion was the religious aspiration of many Christians finding
outlet.

It should not be supposed, however, that the later medieval age
was lacking in true religion of a more mystical and purely
spiritual character. Indeed, it is to this period that Christendom
owes much of the noblest mystical literature of its treasury.
This spiritual movement had its roots in a trio of German
Dominicans, Meister Eckhart of Strasbourg, who died in 1329,
Heinrick Suso of Ulm, who died in 1365, and John Tauler of
Strasbourg, who died in 1361. In the Netherlands it had its
representative in John Ruysbroek, an Augustinian Canon of
Grönendal, near Brussels, the author of the *Theologia Germanica*,
who died in 1381; whilst it reached its finest flowering in the
Imitatio Christi of Thomas à Kempis. Nor was the quest for
immediate knowledge of and communion with God confined to
the examples of outstanding individuals. It found communal
expression in such societies as the Canons Regular of Windes-
heim founded by Gerard Groote, and the semi-lay educational
confraternity of the Brethren of the Common Life, and in the
Gottesfreunde, the Friends of God, in South Germany. Contem-

porary with these mystical writers of the continent were Richard Rolle of Hampole, a religious teacher who was likewise a layman, and Juliana of Norwich, two of the most famous English mystics. If it would be unjust to search the works of these teachers for intimations of unorthodoxy or rebellion, of which indeed they were largely innocent, yet it must be admitted that their doctrine helped in the direction of neglect of the sacramental system of the Church, especially of the ramifications of the Mass. They taught a Way of Devotion, significantly known as the *Devotio Moderna*, which enabled the earnest seeker to establish direct and immediate relationship with God. Such devotional practice, although entirely compatible with regular observance of the religious traditions of the Church, afforded nevertheless a bridge by which more adventurous and dissatisfied spirits passed to hostility to ecclesiastical custom and regulation. Many of the most prominent features of contemporary Catholicism, such as the pleading of the sacrifice of the Mass, the conception of salvation as attained through good works and the consequent necessity of participation in the treasury of merits amassed by the saints, were relegated to the background by these mystical movements. From subordination to elimination, from relegation to rejection, the step was short. Certainly in Germany and the Netherlands there was evident a powerful movement of subjective religious sentiment, which was moreover self-consciously individual and subjective.

An important reinforcement of the tendency towards individualism, observable in many departments of life during the later Middle Ages, was afforded by the popular mystical religious movements. The more restless and discontented spirits amongst their devotees were drawn to a contrast between the direct immediacy of contact with God, with the resultant experience of forgiveness and peace thereby given, and the sacramental and hierarchical system of the Church. Luther's later insistence on Justification by Faith alone was an exaggeration of this element, but its kinship with contemporary mystical tendencies could not be denied. Furthermore, these religious stirrings represented movements unconnected with political causes and were capable of making a widespread popular appeal.

In some movements, as in those of Wyclif and Lollardy in England and of Huss in Bohemia, elements of heresy had definitely been added to opposition and protest, though both Huss and Wyclif began by protest against abuses only, and Huss at his trial maintained his orthodoxy. With his death the religious struggle in Bohemia became inextricably intertwined with racial and nationalist tendencies, and its direct connection with the Reformation movements of the sixteenth century is slight. With Wyclif and Lollardy the case is otherwise. Gregory XI condemned Wyclif as teaching identical doctrines with Marsilius of Padua and John of Jandun (a collaborator of Marsilius and a defender of the Emperor Lewis IV), and from political theories the advance to theological heresy was easy. Nor did Wyclif's movement perish with his death, for his ' poor Preachers ' maintained a fugitive continuity of teaching, despite persecution and suppression, so that when Lutheranism reached England in the early part of Henry VIII's reign, it seemed in some wise a continuation of Lollardy, and was regarded by the episcopate chiefly as an additional incentive to that tendency.

Thus towards the end of the fifteenth century Christian Europe was the scene of many and varied movements of discontent and experiment in religion. There was much popular revulsion from the mechanical and superstitious ideas associated with the Mass, and especially with the multiplication of Masses for the repose of the souls of the departed; and much seeking for a new way of approach to God by some more direct means than through the mediation and intercession of the saints. The old scholastic philosophy had lost its creative and originative power, and was discredited amidst a world of new intellectual stirrings. In many departments of life individualism was marked, and even in the mystical movements of the age subjective religious experience was much lauded. Popular discontent was evident, though as yet lacking direction; whilst among the intellectual circles of society new canons of criticism were being applied to traditional beliefs and practices.

In the sphere of politics and statecraft national kingdoms were approaching their maturity, and rulers were ready to treat the Papacy with scant respect for its exalted claims and prerogatives.

In Spain and France, no less than in England and amongst princes of the Empire, civil rulers were eager to profit from the financial and diplomatic difficulties of the Apostolic See. Meantime the Papacy was caught in the meshes of its own past policy. The tortuous necessities of its Italian diplomacy, the increasing oppressiveness of its financial exactions, the additional cost entailed by its patronage of Renaissance art and letters provoked almost universal disgust. Italianised alike in sentiment and policy, shifting its course amid the constantly-changing currents of international diplomacy, and borne down by the burden of its centralised bureaucracy of officials, it was in no state of readiness to face the forces of religious discontent and intellectual criticism. Leadership in the moral and intellectual spheres could not be expected from it. Yet the end of the Middle Ages was tormented by a manifold dissatisfaction. If the demand for a reform of the Church in head and members should sound in the ears of the Papacy, little hope could be entertained of a vigorous response. And if the demand for reform should be followed by threats of rebellion, the Papacy could look only for defence to those secular kings and princes, with whose predecessors it had negotiated Concordats as the price of its deliverance from the pressure of the Conciliar movement. Upon their fidelity to its cause its hopes must centre. Yet the temptations which beset kings and princes to refashion at least the finances and possessions of the churches within their dominions were strong and seductive. Throughout Western Christendom practical measures of reform were urgently needed, if not long overdue. If the prospect of political advantage should inspire civil rulers to undertake the task, little effective resistance could be anticipated from the episcopate of their several territories, which had been sacrificed by the Papacy to its desire for victory over the Conciliar assemblies. Thus the complex elements, religious, political, social, and intellectual, which combined to fashion the Reformation movements in the various European kingdoms were already present in dissociation. The difficult problem of the student of history is not to discern the ultimate causes of the Reformation nor to explain why it happened, but to trace the particular combination of different factors which moulded its course in the several nations.

Throughout Europe the causes were fundamentally similar. To understand the occasions it is necessary to consider briefly the conditions of countries so different as Germany, Scandinavia, Switzerland, France, England, and Scotland.

CHAPTER II

LUTHERANISM IN GERMANY AND THE
SCANDINAVIAN COUNTRIES

A T the commencement of the sixteenth century, Germany
was vexed by the same ecclesiastical abuses as other
European States, and the so-called *Centum Gravamina* had specified their nature. In addition, however, some evils were exaggerated, and others almost peculiar to Germany. In no country
were cathedral chapters so overtly considered as providing
portions for cadets of noble families, nor bishoprics preserved as
a monopoly of princely households. The lack of such a strong
centralised monarchy as had been fashioned out of conflicting
forces in England, France, and Spain, gave great powers to the
princes, whose nominal subordination to the Emperor detracted
little from their virtual independence. Particularly was Germany
characterised by its great ecclesiastical principalities, embracing
not only important sees but also influential abbeys like that of
Fulda; and by the circumstance that the chief of these ecclesiastical States were immediate, and so maintained their independence of local secular, and to a large measure also of imperial,
control. Their value made them the prey of noble families,
and still worse, they were often held in plurality. One of the
characters whose place in history has been ensured by his association with the Indulgence controversy, Albert of Brandenburg,
was Administrator of the See of Halberstadt and Archbishop of
Magdeburg at the age of twenty-three, and became Archbishop
of Mainz also in the following year. A little later a Bavarian
prince was Archbishop of Cologne, and held four other sees
without having received Priest's Orders. A few of the great sees
preserved freedom of election, notably Trier, whilst their
immediacy saved most from being carried over into Protestantism
by the influence of the civil princes, a fate which befell many of
the mediate bishoprics.

But in general such conditions of plurality led to a lack of episcopal oversight, and left the clergy and laity a prey to their own devices. The close connection between many of the great bishops and the leading princely families made them natural partners in attempts to weaken further the central authority of the emperor. But the political weakness and disunity of Germany should not be over-emphasised. Nor should it be forgotten that the country was still rich and prosperous so far as trade and commerce were concerned, as the wealth and influence of the financial houses testified. Much poverty and social distress existed amongst the class of agricultural peasants, as the subsequent revolts indicated. But the Germany of Charles V was not the ruined, desolated, and poverty-stricken land of the Peace of Westphalia at the end of the Thirty Years' War.

Notwithstanding the combination of circumstances favourable to rebellion, the origin of the German Reformation lay in the religious sphere, and for this reason the career and character of Martin Luther demand some attention if the secret of the movement which received its name from him is to be understood. At the time of the outbreak of the controversy concerning Indulgences he was thirty-four years of age, having been born in 1483. From childhood he evinced a deeply religious temperament, though he was sent to the University of Erfurt to pursue the profession of law. There his oppressive sense of sin drove him, as soon as he had graduated in Arts in 1505, to become a member of the Augustinian Friars, with a view to seeking the salvation of his soul. By the movement of humanism he had been, and continued, little touched, nor had he more than a moderate knowledge of Latin writers and less of Greek. As a friar he became a scholastic theologian of the Nominalist school, to which training he owed much of his later theology. In later life indeed he tended to imagine himself much more original in thought than was in fact the case. Throughout, however, he was intensely set upon working out his own salvation, and with fear and trembling. In this respect he reflected faithfully a dominant tendency of contemporary religion, its widespread terror of death and judgment (for " the wrath of the Lamb " was a favourite subject of mural painting in churches), and its consequent performance of good works in the hope that they would avail for deliverance from purgatory and hell. For this end he had fled from the world to the profession of religion; and to achieve it, he was zealous in fasting, austerity, and confession of sin, until his confessors were wearied by his introspection. Fortunately the Vicar-General of his Order, Staupitz, understood him better; and by recommending to him the study of the German mystics, of the Bible, and of Augustine, contributed greatly to his religious development. It would hardly be an exaggeration to affirm that out of these quarries Luther mined the religious doctrines which were to be stamped upon the later history of the movement called after his name.

Under this triple influence therefore he found the secret which had eluded him hitherto. Over against the sin of Man there stood the righteousness of God, and the love of God must awaken in Man a filial trust which would cast out unconditional and exaggerated fear. To Staupitz Luther owed the thought of the redeeming love of God as the fundamental explanation of the mystery of life; and in the conversions of Augustine and Bernard of Clairvaux he found examples of a conscious assurance of forgiveness and salvation with an attendant happiness and peace, which now became his personal and treasured experience. In interior spiritual experience his religious evolution was almost complete, though it needed much elaboration yet, when in 1508 he was called as professor of philosophy to Wittenberg, the newly-founded university of Frederick the Wise, where he became professor of theology in 1512. His exposition of Biblical and theological themes was practical rather than theoretical, laying stress on the free, unmerited grace of God, upon the impotence of Man's will, upon Predestination, in which respect he was as extreme in opinion as Calvin later, and upon the worthlessness of works as a means of salvation. Gradually he reached the main principles of his theological position, which was later to become rigid under the pressure of controversy, and which rested fundamentally upon his conviction that salvation could be attained only through the recognition of God's power and willingness to effect redemption by the free imputation of His own goodness to those who accept this justification by Faith.

Much medieval precedent could be quoted for the interpretation which Luther put upon Romans i. 17—(" for therein is revealed a righteousness of God by faith unto faith, as it is written, But the righteous shall live by faith ")—as emphasising the importance of faith as an element in justification. Luther's originality lay in his insistence upon justification by faith *alone*, and the implied rejection of all other agents towards salvation. As yet, however, he had disturbed only the proportion of the Faith; for no public issue had arisen to deviate him from the quiet paths of the academy. During this period, indeed, he visited Rome in the spirit of a devout pilgrim, and was shocked by the prevalence of Renaissance and humanistic ideas of conduct there.

The occasion which transformed Luther from an obscure monastic and academic figure into the leader of a widespread German revolt against the Papacy and the traditional ecclesiastical system was the Indulgence controversy of 1517. This public discussion brought the whole doctrine and practice of Indulgence into much popular contempt, from which it is not easy to rescue the matter at this distance of time. Moreover, the principles upon which the practice of indulgences rest are not easily commendable to the modern temper. The Church, as a visible society, with its own discipline for its members, had to grapple with the practical and theoretical aspects of human sinfulness. Sins when committed could be remitted only by repentance, confession, and absolution. But the practical consequences of sin often remained after contrition, confession, and absolution; and the church gave expression to its sense of the social characteristics of sin by imposing penances to be fulfilled as an outward recognition of the hurt suffered by the body of Christ through individual misdoing. Furthermore, the temporal consequences which remained included the time to be spent in Purgatory until each soul was prepared for entrance into Heaven. The custom arose of remitting earthly penances in respect of some special act of faith or charity piously performed, and by a natural process this was extended by Sixtus IV in 1476 to the remission of the consequences of sin in Purgatory. The means by which this could be effected for individual souls was through the Treasury of Merits accumulated by the saints, which could be made available to lighten the satisfaction incumbent upon a sinner in order to make reparation for his sins. In theory therefore an indulgence had no relation to the removal of guilt from the offender, but only affected the temporal consequences of his sin in respect of the penalties to be imposed in this world and after death. Gradually the authority to grant indulgences had been arrogated to itself by the Papacy, and had been used as a means for the relief of its financial necessities. Papal indulgences of varying degrees of operation were issued, the cost being proportionate to the extent and content of the indulgence. The principles upon which the practice of indulgence rested may be illustrated from the *Unigenitus Dei filius* of Pope Clement VI in 1343, which explained how the sacrifice of Christ had established an ' infinitus thesaurus ' for men, the administration of which had been committed by God to the see of Peter.

> Quem quidem thesaurum . . . per beatum Petrum coelo clavigerum, eiusque successores suos in terris vicarios, commisit fidelibus salubriter dispensandum et propriis et rationabilibus causis, nunc pro totali, nunc pro partiali remissione poenae temporalibus pro peccatis debitae, tam generaliter quam specialiter (prout cum Deo expedire cognoscerent) vere poenitentibus et confessis misericorditer applicandum.[1]

Thus indulgences were restricted to the penalties imposed for sins, for which either a complete or partial remission could be granted, and the effectiveness was conditioned by the repentance and confession of the sinner. Undoubtedly the most serious examples of indulgence were those of plenary character, such as that granted by Boniface VIII in 1300 to mark the proclamation of the famous Jubilee, by which pilgrims to Rome, who had duly repented and confessed, were given " non solum plenam et largiorem, imo plenissimam omnium suorum . . . veniam peccatorum ". Other indulgences might be of limited scope, being granted on the occasion of the consecration of a church, or

---

[1] Which treasury He gave to be dispensed for their salvation to the faithful through blessed Peter (who holds the keys of heaven) and through his successors and vicars on earth; and, for due and proper reasons, to be applied to those who truly repent and humbly confess, for remission of the penalties due for temporal sins, either partial or total remission, either general or restricted, as under God they shall deem expedient.

attached to a particular altar in a church or chapel, and of temporary duration. Indulgences were generally brought to the
notice of the common people by the itinerary of an appointed
preacher and vendor, carrying the original bull of indulgence,
travelling in state, and proclaiming its merits in the several towns
through which his route lay. Probably the invention of printing
did much to extend the practice and increase the number of
copies sold; and the friars, as Chaucer testified, were often
amongst the foremost and most zealous dealers in indulgences.

The indulgence which provoked Luther's famous theses illustrated well the disastrous consequences of financial and commercial trafficking in spiritual concerns. The object of the sale was
to provide for a pressing papal objective. Nicholas V had begun
the destruction of St. Peter's at Rome about the middle of the
fifteenth century, and Julius II issued an indulgence for the work
of its rebuilding, which was continued by Leo X. At this
juncture the indulgence became connected with the ecclesiastical
fortunes of Albert of Brandenburg, who had secured election to
the archbishopric of Mainz. He was a prelate indeed of distinctly
secular tastes and Renaissance morals (his mistresses even riding
in male attire), and his election to this see in his twenty-fifth
year was sufficiently significant, apart from his desire to retain
also the sees of Magdeburg and Halberstadt. After long nego-
tiation Leo X consented, and Albert was required to pay for his
confirmation in these sees a fee of 14,000 ducats, besides the
extraordinary tax of 10,000 ducats for holding the two extra
bishoprics in addition to Mainz. The historian of the popes, Dr.
Pastor, though not regarding the transaction as simoniacal, considered it " a disgraceful affair for all concerned "; and its consequences were certainly disastrous. The large sum promised by
Albert was advanced by the banking house of Fugger, and, to
enable the archbishop to repay his creditors, the pope allowed
him to proclaim the indulgence in his ecclesiastical jurisdiction
and in the territories of his brother, the Elector Joachim of
Brandenburg. Half the proceeds were to go towards the rebuilding of St. Peter's, and half to Albert himself. Thus was the
indulgence compassed about with financial conditions, due to
the difficulties of pope and prelate. It was a plenary indulgence,

the benefits of which extended to the dead in purgatory as well
as to the quick, so that a wide sale was anticipated.

The preacher of the indulgence in the territories of Albert
and Joachim of Brandenburg was John Tetzel, a Dominican,
whose eloquence commended it widely. So far as concerned its
application to the living, his preaching was in accord with
official doctrine. But in respect of the dead, in the judgment
of Pastor,

> there is no doubt that Tetzel did . . . proclaim as Christian doctrine that
> nothing but an offering of money was required to gain the indulgence
> for the dead, without there being any question of contrition or confes-
> sion. He also taught, in accordance with the opinion then held, that an
> indulgence could be applied to any given soul with unfailing effect.
> Starting from this assumption, there is no doubt that his doctrine was
> virtually that of the drastic proverb:
>
> > ' As soon as money in the coffer rings,
> > The soul from purgatory's fire springs.'
>
> The papal bull of indulgence gave no sanction whatever to this pro-
> position.

The proclamation of the indulgence was not allowed in Saxony,
but the people of Wittenberg were able to make the easy
journey to Jutterbog to receive copies, and from this incident
sprang the controversy which brought Luther from obscurity
into the centre of the stage of Germany, and shortly of Europe
also.

On 31st October, 1517, Luther affixed to the door of the
castle-church at Wittenberg ninety-five theses, challenging to a
dispute on the question of indulgences. The theses were written
in Latin and in the usual scholastic form, so that their issue might
appear no more than a dispute between an Augustinian Friar and
a Dominican, which might develop at worst into the propor-
tions of the controversy which the Dominicans of Cologne had
waged against the Hebrew studies of Reuchlin. Beneath the
conventional forms of theological disputation, however, Luther
had hidden the fire of revolution. His first proposition declared
that Christ had ' intended that the whole life of believers should
be penitence ', the thirty-sixth affirmed that every Christian who
feels true compunction has plenary remission of penalty and

guilt without letters of pardon, whilst the fifty-eighth formally denied the ecclesiastical doctrine of the treasury of merits. Despite the indignation aroused in Luther by the indulgence preached by Tetzel, he had as yet no intention of separating himself from the Church. Nor, if his theses had remained a subject of interest in academic circles only, might that possibility have become a probability, and then an accomplished fact. Attempts indeed were made to heal the breach, during the exchange of controversial writings, into the details of which it is not necessary to enter. In July 1518 Luther was summoned to Rome, but instead Cardinal Cajetan was given authority to deal with the case at Augsburg. Thither Luther repaired, and conferences were held with Cajetan which, though friendly in tone, could hardly be other than sterile, since Luther was required to recant his opinions, not to justify them in argument. Accordingly he left Augsburg, appealing from the pope badly-informed to a future pope better-informed, an appeal which was afterwards enlarged to one from the pope to a general council.

Meanwhile the dispute had assumed a wider significance and was being extended in scope to embrace many subjects besides that of indulgences. The fire which had burned beneath the scholastic theses spread, and despite their academic form, they became a signal for an almost national German revolt against the Papacy and the existing ecclesiastical system. Translated into German and printed in thousands, they became the focus of a widespread discontent, though this dissatisfaction proceeded from a variety of differing motives. Such at least was the fact; for the protest against indulgences swelled into Protestantism. The explanation of the success and popularity of Luther's theses is more difficult to essay. That which best fits the facts is a recognition of the widespread revulsion from the Church and its system, alike in its theological and its financial expression The old order in Germany, as in the political sphere in France in 1789, though outwardly imposing and strong, was rotten inwardly, and collapsed before the first sharp impact of revolt. Beneath the controversy about indulgences was concealed on the religious and theological side a growing persuasion of the reality of justification by faith alone, of the impotence of the human

will to work out its own salvation with fear and trembling, of
the inefficacy of the system of good works and of the treasury
of merits proclaimed and administered by the Church, and therefore ultimately a doubt of the necessity of either Church or
Sacraments to salvation. Luther himself found the grounds of his
theological protest widening under pressure of discussion, into
which he was drawn by Dr. Eck; and where he led many
followed. Added to the religious questions were the complex
problems associated with the Curia and its judicial and financial administration. It says much for the unpopularity of Papacy
and Church in Germany that Luther's action brought down so
much of its traditional organisation.

Other factors, too, were ready to join in the struggle. Political
ambitions of the princes of the empire lent an immediate, though
problematical, support to Luther; and social grievances on the
part of the peasantry were awakened into active movement.
Luther himself in 1520 gave a great impetus to the tendencies
towards revolt by the publication of his three most famous
popular writings, the *Address to the Nobility of the German Nation*,
Concerning Christian Liberty, and *On the Babylonish Captivity of
the Church*. With this step he established his reputation as a
redoubtable pamphleteer, and set his feet firmly upon the road
towards repudiation of the traditional church system in all its
works. The first of these pamphlets provided a rallying point
for all criticism and discontent and adumbrated a definite programme of action. It attacked the traditional conception of the
spiritual estate as a corporation of bishops and clergy by affirming the priesthood of all believers, by explaining the clerical
order as differing from the laity only in function, and by denying
that ordination conferred an indelible character. Next it proceeded to refute the propositions that the Papacy was the
authoritative interpreter of the Scriptures, and that the Papacy
alone could summon a council. Instead Luther called upon the
temporal power to resume the authority exercised by the Christian emperors of convoking a general council to undertake the
work of reformation. Objects of reform were easily specified, in
the worldly splendour of the Curia, the financial spoliation and
exploitation of Germany through a variety of expedients and

the pamphlet concluded with suggestions for religious reform, abolishing the papal supremacy in Germany, restricting pilgrimages, allowing the revocation of monastic vows and the marriage of the clergy, and restricting, if not making a complete end of, Masses for the dead, holy days, and veneration of the saints. Luther had travelled far from the dispute concerning the proper theological doctrine of indulgences, and had laid the axe to the roots of the medieval faith and practice. The *Address to the Nobility of the German Nation* was the most important of the three popular writings, because of its practical character. The others expounded the religious basis of these demands for reform, and in particular the tract *On the Babylonish Captivity of the Church* dealt with each of the seven Sacraments, demanding specifically the restoration of the Cup to the laity, denying the doctrine of Transubstantiation, and attacking the multiplication of Masses for the dead and the belief out of which they had grown that the Mass is a good work and a sacrifice.

After the circulation of these pamphlets, reconciliation with the ecclesiastical authorities was hardly to be expected, and the issue of the bull of excommunication of Luther by Leo X on 15th June, 1520, under the title *Exsurge Domine*, was little more than an acknowledgment of the situation already existing. More important from Luther's standpoint and from the position accepted in his *Address to the Nobility of the German Nation* was the attitude to be adopted by the new Emperor, Charles V, who had succeeded in the previous year to the imperial dignity. This unfortunate young prince inherited great possessions, and with them greater difficulties. As Holy Roman Emperor he was the defender of the Church and suppressor of heresy; and the championship of orthodoxy was congenial to his personal desire, as he declared at Worms. But his claims and influence in Italy made him oft-times the political enemy of the Papacy, whose ecclesiastical ally he was. Moreover, his dynastic rivalry with France impelled French kings, zealous in the persecution of heresy within their own dominions, to make alliance with the forces of Protestantism in Germany, and even to reach an understanding with the foe of all Christian princes, Suleiman the Magnificent of Turkey. Compassed on all sides by political rivalries, Charles could never free his hands to deal with the religious problem in Germany. Nor was the majority of the princes of the empire, even of those who remained loyal to the ancient faith, willing to allow him under the pretext of enforcing religious unity against heresy to strengthen the imperial authority and reduce their political power. Despite the strong declaration of Charles at the Diet of Worms in 1521 and the decree of the diet putting Luther to the imperial ban, and forbidding his works and teaching, it was impossible to suppress his movement. A few years later the Diet of Speier in 1526 resolved that in matters of religion each ruler should so " live, govern, and carry himself as he hoped and trusted to answer it to God and His Imperial Majesty ". The principle which was to receive formal acceptance at the Peace of Augsburg in 1555, that of *cujus regio ejus religio*, was adumbrated at Speier, and speedily acted upon. The political repercussions of Lutheranism in Germany were complex and protracted, resulting in the division of the princes into two camps, whose military fortunes fluctuated considerably. Luther's reliance upon the princes was emphasised by his attitude towards the social rebellions known as the Peasants' Revolt of 1524, which were the product of such religious and apocalyptic teachings as prevailed in Cromwell's army in seventeenth-century England. Much genuine religious zeal and more social discontent lay at the root of these uprisings; but Luther refused utterly to compromise his religious reformation by association with social revolution. Supporting the princes in their most extreme measures of repression, he earned in return their championship of his cause, which was bound the more closely to their interests and authority.

Despite its relations with political and social movements, Lutheranism remained fundamentally a religious movement. To the papal bull of excommunication Luther replied with a symbolic act of defiance by his burning of the bull together with volumes of the canon law and scholastic theology, and with a declaration *Adversus execrabilem Anti-Christi bullam*, an identification of the Pope with Anti-Christ which Lord Acton regarded as marking the final breach with Rome. His movement continued to gather support from the widespread antipathy to the

Papacy throughout Germany, as the papal legate to the Diet of Worms, Aleander, recognised in his admission that "nine out of every ten cry 'Luther', and the tenth, if he do not care for what Luther says, at least cries, 'Death to the Court of Rome', and everyone demands and shrieks, 'Council! Council!'". The greater part of this popular feeling was negative in character, and it is impossible to establish a religious movement solely upon negatives. Luther therefore had to hammer out a positive and constructive programme for himself and his followers in the spheres of both faith and practice. The execution of this difficult task was rendered more difficult by the constant pressure of external disputes in the field of political events, and by the internal controversies which attended the opening of the flood-gates of religious pamphleteering. Despite these unfavourable circumstances, the work was urgent and necessary; and beneath the dust and clamour of controversy it is possible to discern the main features of Lutheranism in religious practice, belief, and church order.

After the decree of Worms Luther returned to an honourable and entirely safe captivity in the Wartburg, where he began his translation into German of the New Testament, 1522, followed by the Old Testament, which he completed only in 1534. It would be difficult to overestimate the importance and influence of Luther's provision of the Holy Bible in the vernacular both from the standpoint of the establishment of his own movement and from that of the religious history of Germany. In its influence upon religion and language it is comparable with the English Bible. It brought Luther even more into touch with national sentiment, it set the standard of German literary language, and it provided an indispensable foundation for the religious life, public worship, and domestic piety of the adherents of his movement. Though in the intimate sphere of private devotion and belief, the influence of Luther's Bible may be imponderable and intangible, its importance is self-evident. Together with the Holy Scriptures went out a volume of pamphlets and tracts, and, second in weight to the vernacular Bible only, stand the hymns which formed one of the most remarkable literary products of the Lutheran movement. The importance of hymnody in religious revivals is demonstrated abundantly by the history of the Methodist movement in eighteenth-century England; and the place occupied in that revival by the hymns of Charles Wesley was taken in sixteenth-century Germany by the hymns of Luther and his followers. A veritable school of hymn-writers arose, led by Luther himself, who, perceiving the need of a vernacular hymnody, set to work to supply the lack. To such collections as the *Erfurter Enchiridion* and the *Chorgesangbüchlein* he was the chief contributor; and of his own thirty-six hymns, twenty-four are traceable to the years 1523-4. Not without reason did Heine call the greatest of his hymns, *Ein' feste Burg ist unser Gott*, the Marseillaise of the Reformation. No estimate of the religious significance of Lutheranism which fails to give high place to the German Bible and its evangelical hymn-books can offer an adequate explanation of its character and appeal.

The enduring character of a religious movement must depend, however, not less upon its appeal to the head than to the heart; and the provision of a vernacular Bible and of popular hymns was an inadequate basis upon which to build a rival to the medieval ecclesiastical system. Theology was still considered as the science of ultimate Reality; and theologians were expected to speak with authority upon those beliefs which a Christian man must hold and profess for his soul's health. Luther had been in origin an earnest seeker for salvation; and if his rebellion against Rome and its system of belief and practice were to possess staying power, it must needs have both a theology and a liturgy. Nor, if Luther had been oblivious to this necessity, would the pressure of events have allowed him to elude it. The intellectual atmosphere of the age, especially in the universities, was too charged with novel speculations and strange doctrines to permit the challenge to be evaded. The discrediting of the Thomist scholasticism, the influence of Renaissance humanism, the problem of the interpretation of the Bible, and the authority to be attached to the traditional conciliar theological definitions, all made imperative the framing of a system of sound doctrine. Yet for this task Luther was not well fitted by temperament or training. The defects of his education and the limitations of his

learning made him ill-equipped for the task of proclaiming a
new theology. Nor did the polemics which he exchanged with
such radical teachers as Carlstadt, Pfeiffer, and Münzer produce
a state of intellectual calm suitable to the careful pondering of
fundamental theological questions. In face of such extremists,
indeed, Luther's innate conservatism emerged into prominence.
The opening of the indulgence dispute had found him with no
idea of breaking away from the church in which he had been
taught and reared; nor had his mind explored the implications
of his attack upon the system of the Treasury of Merits, the use
of private Masses, and the relation of works to faith. His subsequent steps had been taken rapidly and under pressure of dis-
turbing conditions; but he retained to the end a stubborn
conservatism.

In sacramental doctrine, which was the storm-centre of theological discussion, he clung tenaciously to the belief in a real and
bodily presence of Christ in the Holy Eucharist. Transubstantiation he rejected as philosophically unsound and unsatisfying;
but this was only the form in which the vital truth to which
he held had been expressed. His own alternative, Consubstan-
tiation, endeavoured to retain belief in the real presence of the
body and blood of Christ by affirming that the Elements after
consecration possessed the substance of Christ's body and blood
in addition to their natural substance of bread and wine, thereby
endowing them with two substances. As a philosophical interpretation it was subject to criticism as vulnerable as that which
he had himself directed against Transubstantiation. But for the
truth underlying both interpretations he contended with unyielding firmness against both Carlstadt and Zwingli and their
followers; and the tenth article of the Confession of Augsburg,
1530, affirmed *De Coena Domini docent, quod corpus et sanguis
Christi vere adsint.*

As with the doctrine of the Eucharist, so in respect of its
celebration Luther clung to traditional customs, such as the
crucifix, candles, and the Mass vestments; and Lutheran conservatism in these matters was to shock the Anglican chaplain who
accompanied George I on his first visit to Hanover in 1716, so
that he wondered " how far the English there might be scan-

dalised at the crucifix on the altar and the many images in the Lutheran churches ", assuring the archbishop of Canterbury that he had seen not only crucifixes and images but also " in tablets carved and painted the whole Popish history of the Virgin Mary ". In his *Formula Missae et Communionis* of 1523 and in the German *Mass and Order of Divine Service* of 1526, Luther preserved a liturgical Office, embracing Introit, Kyrie eleison, Epistle, Gradual, Gospel, Nicene Creed, sermon, exhortation and Lord's Prayer, a prayer of Consecration which included only the words of Institution taken from 1 Corinthians xi, the elevation and Sanctus, concluding with a collect and blessing. It was his desire that Mass should be celebrated, with a sermon on the Gospel for the day, each Sunday. In all matters concerning the Eucharist, indeed, Luther was characterised by a conservatism which some of his followers found difficult to tolerate.

The task of framing a new theology, for which Luther's abilities did not well fit him, fell to the lot of his disciple, Philip Melanchthon, who possessed, indeed, nearly all the qualities requisite for that undertaking. A youthful prodigy, who had graduated B.A. at Heidelberg at the age of fourteen, Melanchthon had declined already an invitation to become a professor at Ingolstadt (later to become a leader in the Counter-reformation movement against Lutheranism), before accepting one to Wittenberg to the chair of Greek when he was still only twenty-one years of age in 1518. There he fell naturally under Luther's influence, and, possessing a natural inclination towards theology and the scholar's distaste for inchoate and extreme opinions, he proceeded to construct a positive, moderate, and persuasive theological basis for the new movement. In 1521 appeared his *Loci Communes*, which has been not unworthily called the first Protestant system of theology; and he was largely responsible for the Confession of Augsburg of 1530, consisting of twenty-one articles of faith and seven additional articles upon abuses to be reformed. Upon this Confession the doctrinal standards of Lutheranism were based. The most important articles were the fourth, affirming justification by faith alone, the sixth, asserting that faith had good works as its fruit, which every man was bound to perform though not as a means of salvation, the

seventh, accepting belief in the Holy Catholic Church, but
defining the church as a congregation of the faithful, in which
the Gospel is rightly preached and the Sacraments rightly
administered, the ninth, tenth, and eleventh, which accepted
the Sacraments of Baptism and the Lord's Supper, and retained
the use of private confession, and the thirteenth, which defined
sacraments as *signa et testimonia voluntatis Dei erga nos, ad excitan-
dam et confirmandam fidem*. Amongst the abuses noted as needing
reformation were the denial of the chalice to the laity, the
celibacy of the clergy, the Mass conceived as *opus delens peccata
vivorum et mortuorum ex opere operato*, the excessive number of
ceremonies, the institution of monastic vows, and abuses of
ecclesiastical power, especially of episcopal authority, and the
necessity of distinguishing it from the civil authority upon which
it so often encroached. The relative moderation of this Confession and the awakening realisation on the part of Rome of
the gravity of the developing schism led to a series of eirenical
conferences between representatives of all sides; of which the
most promising was that held at Ratisbon in 1541, attended by
Cardinal Contarini as papal legate, at which agreement was
reached about Justification (though the form of words was
rejected by the Consistory at Rome) and about Ordination,
Baptism, and Confirmation, though in the questions relating to
the Mass, Absolution, and clerical celibacy, agreement was not
possible. Notwithstanding the failure of attempts at compromise, Melanchthon and the Augsburg Confession provided
Lutheranism with a doctrinal statement, based upon Scripture,
and moderate in character.

There remained the practical problem of Church Order in the
new communities; and in the working out of a system of church
government, political exigencies naturally exercised a dominating influence. It has been much disputed whether Luther
originally held that the Prince, or chief magistrate, was always
by virtue of his civil office the rightful ruler of the church, or
whether he taught that under certain circumstances, then in
existence, the Prince was the most suitable person to whom the
Christian community should delegate the exercise of that
authority of government which its members corporately pos-

sessed. Luther, indeed, had appealed to the temporal power to resume the authority of the Christian Roman emperors to summon a general council for the reform of the Church. In Germany, however, the Emperor Charles V was the ally of the Papacy. If reform was to be effected there, the initiative must be taken by the several princes within their own dominions, pending the time when the emperor would convoke a General Council, and the whole Church would thereby be purified and corrected. The logic and practice were natural, therefore, which led princes and free cities to undertake the responsibility of reform; and the result was inevitable that Lutheranism should depend still more upon the support of the civil prince. A number of reformations resulted in Germany, though characterised by common features. Generally the civil rulers took advantage of the occasion to make an end of monasteries, monastic orders, and mediate bishoprics. The way was shown by a prince outside the boundaries of the empire, the Margrave Albert of Brandenburg, Grand Master of the Teutonic Order, who married, secularised the territories of the Order, and received them back as an hereditary dukedom under the suzerainty of Poland in 1525. The two bishops of his territories, the Bishops of Samland and Pomerania, followed his example and by commission from him carried through a programme of reform. Within the empire the Elector of Saxony began the task. Four commissions of laymen and clergy visited four divisions of the electorate, aided by a series of Instructions to Visitors drawn up by Melanchthon. Other princes, and free cities, copied the example set; and by this initiative the princes secured the control and direction of ecclesiastical policy, exercising the authority and in some cases, as in Prussia, assuming the title of *summepiskopat*.

The Confession of Augsburg had used moderate and guarded language of the episcopal office, protesting rather against the confusion of civil with ecclesiastical power than against the spiritual authority of the episcopate; and the Instructions to Visitors in Saxony in 1528 referred to the desire of the Reformers " to bring back the true office of bishops and visitation ". In practice, however, the traditional conception of the bishop as constituting a separate Order of the Christian ministry was abandoned; and the Lutheran church admitted only one Order of Ministry. The existence of Superintendents, each with a territorial district subject to his oversight, was indeed recognised; but the difference was one of administration and function, not of Order or grade in the ministry. Even where Superintendents came to assume the title of Bishop, there was no conception of a separate and higher Order. Wittenberg furnished a supply of zealous reforming ministers; but generally the existing clergy remained in possession under the new régime. The princes assumed to themselves the ecclesiastical patronage which had been formerly in the possession of bishops and of clerical corporations, though the force of tradition proved too strong to enable them to break the lay patronage exercised by the lords of the manor. The civil power likewise arrogated to itself a considerable authority in prescribing the liturgical order of service to be used; whilst it secured the provision of a succession of clergy by the encouragement of theological faculties in the universities. Through the organisation also of a ministry of cult, associated generally with the direction of education, the temporal authority found its control over both church and schools usefully exercised. Thus the Lutheran system established itself under the benign protection of the princes and free cities. On the whole it functioned effectually and smoothly, offering to its adherents an ordered system of belief and practice, based upon the Word of God. Its official ministry, like that of the Methodist Church organised by John Wesley in eighteenth-century England, offered few prizes, and was recruited mainly from the middle classes of society. With the secularisation of episcopal property, indeed, the temptation to cadets of princely families to enter upon an ecclesiastical career was removed; but though the Lutheran ministry generally did not attract persons of high position to its service, it ministered faithfully to the needs of those who sought in the new system an alternative to the Roman faith and practice. With the formal recognition of the principle of *cujus regio, ejus religio* at the Peace of Augsburg in 1555, the first stage in the history of the Lutheran reforming movement in Germany was attained.

Meanwhile Lutheranism had spread beyond Germany, and

was destined to exercise an important influence on the Reformation movements in the Scandinavian countries around the Baltic Sea. Here the religious changes were inextricably entangled with political events, much after the manner of developments in contemporary England. The Danish king was still nominally ruler over Sweden and Norway also, though in actual fact Sweden was already advancing towards independence. Christian II, married to Isabella, sister of the Emperor Charles V, took up the anti-clerical side of the Reformation for political reasons and endeavoured to use it to the profit of the monarchy against both nobles and clergy. His cruelty and unpopularity led to his deposition in 1523 by his uncle, Frederick, Duke of Schleswig-Holstein, in whose duchy Lutheranism was already powerful. The breach with Rome had its immediate occasion in a disputed election to the archbishopric of Lund in 1519, the consequences of which were serious. Henceforth no Danish bishop sought confirmation of his election from the Papacy, but from the crown, to which also the customary fees were paid, and the new bishops remained unconsecrated, so that the episcopal succession in Denmark was lost. The new royal dynasty was definitely associated with the Reformation movement, for Frederick married his daughter to Albert of Brandenburg, and his son, who succeeded him as Christian III, was a definite Lutheran. Despite episcopal opposition, Frederick carried an Ordinance of the Diet of Odense in 1527 by which royal protection was granted to Lutherans, marriage of clergy was authorised, and bishops were required to seek confirmation from the crown instead of from Rome. The progress of reforming doctrines was assisted by the influx of Lutherans from Wittenberg, of both German and Danish extraction, by the patronage accorded to Hans Tausen, the 'Danish Luther', by Frederick, who made him his chaplain, and by the translation into Danish of the New Testament in 1524. After Frederick's death, however, much conflict ensued before Christian III finally achieved his own triumph and that of the Reformation. In 1536 episcopacy was abolished, ecclesiastical lands were confiscated to the crown, and Bugenhagen, who had already organised Lutheranism in Pomerania, was called in to draft a new church constitution.

In 1537 he arrived, crowned the king and queen, and began the work of reorganisation by laying hands upon seven men to discharge the office of superintendents, with the title and territorial designation of bishops. To assist them in their administration rural deans were elected, though the financial control of the confiscated church property was retained by royal officials. There followed a Church Ordinance authorising forms of public worship of characteristic Lutheran conservatism, and a reconstitution of the University of Copenhagen with three professors of the Old and New Testaments respectively, and of Lutheran doctrines. Thus Denmark was Lutheranised, and the process of reformation was extended to Norway with the accompaniment of considerable violence. Political independence and the traditional ecclesiastical system disappeared together, and Iceland also was compelled to accept the Lutheran Church.

In Sweden the Reformation was effected not by the domination of Denmark but by the rise to power and to the royal title of the Vasa family, the creators of Swedish independence. Christian II had forfeited popularity in Sweden by the ' Stockholm blood-bath ' of 1520, in which some hundreds of leading ecclesiastics and nobles were massacred, and Gustavus Vasa headed a national revolt, securing the title of king in 1523. The office to which he was thus elected presented more difficulties than strength, and particularly the poverty of the crown contrasted markedly with the wealth of the Church and its episcopate. The Swedish episcopate was to a considerable degree the preserve of the leading noble families, and the advance of the crown to power could only be attained by the subjugation of these rivals. Both political and financial motives prompted Gustavus Vasa to champion the Reformation, and at the Riksdag of Westerås in 1527 he made serious demands for the alienation of ecclesiastical property to the crown. The threatened bishops appealed for support to Rome; but the king brought matters to a decision by a threat of resignation of the throne. Accordingly the opposition gave way, and the Ordinances of Westerås placed all monastic, capitular, and episcopal lands at the king's disposal for confiscation or religious use. Meanwhile Lutheran influences had penetrated the country, especially through the teaching of two Swedish students from Wittenberg, Olaf and Lars Peterssen. The Riksdag at Westerås, therefore, decreed that preachers henceforth should set forth only the pure Word of God (though no theological definition of this standard was issued), that all priests should be subject to civil jurisdiction, and that all church offices should be awarded only with the royal consent.

The Swedish Church was thus set on the road towards Lutheranism, though the name was never adopted, and the reformed church still bears the simple designation of " the Church of Sweden ". The episcopal succession moreover was carefully preserved. In 1524 the appointment of Petrus Magni to be Bishop of Westerås had been confirmed by the Papacy, and Petrus had been consecrated to the episcopate in Rome. He consecrated three bishops for the reformed Swedish Church, including an archbishop of Upsala, and crowned Gustavus. In 1531 the Swedish Mass Book, Lutheran in doctrine and structure, was published, followed by the Swedish Bible, including the Apocrypha, in 1541. Compulsory auricular confession had been abolished at Westerås, and the reformed church proceeded along Lutheran lines, though without any formal adoption of its official confession of faith. As the reforming movement had been profoundly influenced in its origins by royal policy, so its development was affected by the same factor. The successor of Gustavus, Eric XIV, inclined to Calvinism, whilst his successor, John III, in turn manifested more Catholic leanings, and the possibility of reconciliation with Rome might have been envisaged if the Papacy had been ready for compromise on such matters as the marriage of the clergy and a vernacular liturgy. More significant was the fact that John's son, Sigismund, heir also to the throne of Poland, had been brought up in the Roman Catholic faith, so that when he succeeded to the Swedish throne in 1592 his uncle, who acted as regent and afterwards secured the crown as Charles IX, summoned a synod at Upsala to define formally the faith and practice of the Swedish Church. At this synod the Confession of Augsburg was adopted in its unaltered form of 1530. The basis of doctrine was declared to be the Bible, and assent was given to the three Catholic creeds. In matters of ceremonies, the Swedish Church retained many symbols of the old order, both in respect of vestments and ceremonial acts. No martyrs for the Roman obedience were forthcoming, and the proportion of dissent from the Swedish Church was, and has remained, negligible.

The first-fruits of the revolt against Rome, therefore, were seen in the widespread establishment of Lutheran churches, characterised by insistence on the preaching of the Word of God, the experience of justifying faith, the rejection of private Masses offered for the quick and the dead, and the prominence of an individual and personal religious experience. Except in Sweden the episcopal form of government was abandoned and the succession broken. Generally, however, Lutheranism was the most conservative movement of the Continental reformation. Geographically it established itself within the Empire in Saxony, Hesse, and most of Lower Germany, with Würtemberg in the midst of the Roman Catholic south and in Bohemia; and outside the Empire in the Scandinavian lands, Poland, including Polish Prussia, Eastern Prussia, Curland, Livonia, Esthonia, Hungary, and in Transylvania.

CHAPTER III

ZWINGLI, CALVIN, AND THE REFORMED CHURCHES

FEW countries of sixteenth-century Europe presented a more promising field for the influence of the Reformation movement than Switzerland, where the sense of unity was weak both in the political and ecclesiastical spheres. The national unity of Switzerland was not accorded formal recognition indeed until 1648, and meanwhile the Federal tie between its several country and city cantons was slight. Ecclesiastically the five Swiss dioceses were all subject to the jurisdiction of foreign metropolitans, those of Constance and Coire to Mainz, those of Basle and Lausanne to Besançon, and that of Sion to Tarantaise until its emancipation at the hands of Leo X. This lack of unity in organisation was accompanied by a general absence of effective episcopal oversight. The influential city of Zurich, for example, was in the diocese of Constance, whose distant bishop exercised little supervision over its clergy. Generally the standard of clerical morality was low, and ecclesiastical issues were closely bound up with the jealousy felt by the leading cities for their episcopal superiors. The division between Romance or French Switzerland and Teutonic or German Switzerland also opened the country to a variety of religious influences, and in turn enabled it to influence religious developments both in the Empire and in France. The presence of so many elements antecedently favourable to the Reformation movement made Switzerland a centre of religious influence second in importance to no other European State.

The beginnings of the Reformation in Switzerland were associated with the city of Zurich and the career of Zwingli. Huldreich (or Ulrich) Zwingli was a contemporary of Luther, having been born in 1484, but unlike the German reformer, was profoundly influenced by the humanist tendencies of the age. In his case this influence extended to the sphere of personal morality, thus differentiating him sharply from his master in

49

intellectual studies, Erasmus. Like Erasmus he studied the Greek Patristic writings, and the Greek New Testament, and learned some Hebrew for the better understanding of the Old Testament. His early studies at Basle, Berne, and Vienna brought him under powerful humanist influences, which moulded the entire pattern of his thought. Before becoming famous as a leader of reform at Zurich he had a varied and adventurous career. He was a secular priest at Glarus, whence he travelled thrice to Italy as chaplain to mercenaries from Glarus employed in the papal service in the Italian wars. In return for these services he received in 1513 a papal pension. In 1516 he removed as parish priest to Einsiedeln, having brought opposition upon himself at Glarus by his criticism of the hiring of Swiss soldiers as mercenaries by France. At Einsiedeln his satirical observations upon pardoners and indulgences did not provoke the papal wrath, since in 1518 he was made Acolyte Chaplain to the pope. In the same year, however, came the momentous change in his life, when he was elected in December to the office of people's priest in the Great Minster at Zurich. Here he secured a rapid reputation as a preacher, and embarked upon that course which was to lead to his repudiation of the traditional system of religious belief and practice in a manner far more thoroughgoing and radical than that of Luther.

Zwingli, indeed, was essentially a teacher and lecturer, who interpreted the work of the Christian ministry chiefly as that of instruction and education. Though not devoid of personal religious experience, his interest was always rather in sound and rational belief than in any mystical apprehension of God. He studied and expounded the Scriptures, but without reference to any authority external to the Bible and the individual conscience. The Scriptures were not only to be the subject of unfettered intellectual study, but were also to be interpreted according to the opinion of each individual. This did not imply, of course, that Zwingli had any doubt concerning the final authority of Scripture as the basis of doctrine, but only that he relied completely upon individual interpretation to elucidate its meaning without the help of any other authority. Thus it came to pass that Zwingli gave a prominence unusual even amongst the

Reformers to the pulpit as the vehicle of Christian worship, and to the exposition of the Word of God as the central feature of divine service. In Zurich he found a city enjoying an unusual degree of jurisdiction over its clergy, and affording therefore an invaluable practical basis for reform. At first his preaching was directed against obvious abuses, such as provoked the protests of Luther, though Zwingli's action was quite independent of that of his German contemporary. When the same indulgence which provoked Luther's theses was attacked in Zurich, papal consideration for its own dependence upon Swiss military help caused the withdrawal of the indulgence. From this beginning Zwingli went on to attack other points, both ecclesiastical and political. In the political sphere he opposed the selling of their services as mercenary troops by the Swiss, resigning his papal pension in order to lend consistency to his protest, and persuading Zurich in 1521 to prohibit the mercenary system. In religion he attacked monastic vows, the compulsory exaction of tithe, the observance of the Lenten fast, and the invocation of Saints. Thus doctrinal and political questions became blended, for Zwingli realised fully the necessity to his success of the support of the city, so that the reformation carried through at Zurich embraced both the political aspect of a revolt of the city against the control of the distant Bishop of Constance and a radical religious remodelling of the belief and worship of the Christian community.

Secure in the support of the Great Council of the city Zwingli directed the course of the reforming movement, beginning in 1522 with the allowance of clerical marriage, the abolition of images and relics, and the disuse of traditional ceremonies, and culminating in the suppression and secularisation of the monasteries, the diversion of their revenues to educational purposes, the reconstitution of the Great Minster, and the substitution of the German *Action oder Bruch des Nachtmals* for the Latin Mass in 1525. In the matter of externals, he swept away all signs of the ancient order, not only images, relics, pictures, and pilgrimages, but even organs being abolished as hindrances to the proper understanding of the true Christian faith, which should be learned by study of the Bible and hearing of sermons. In the new Order for the Communion it was decreed that the bread should " be carried round by the appointed ministers on large wooden tranchers from one seat to the next " amongst the worshippers, and the wine likewise in wooden beakers, so that " no pomp come back again " into the service. Public disputations were held and printed tracts widely distributed to ensure the popular understanding of the principles at issue. The sole authority for Christian doctrine and practice was declared to be the Word of God, and the sufficient authority for the practical carrying out of the reforms was the Town Council. Thus the Council enforced attendance at public worship and conformity to the new régime on all its citizens. The protests of the Bishop of Constance were naturally unheeded, since the city was resolved to reject his control; but greater trouble was occasioned by the Anabaptists who, emerging from the circle of Zwingli's most ardent followers and supporters, wished to proceed beyond the limits prescribed by their whilom leader. Anabaptism was the *bête noire* of all the Reformers, and its representatives at Zurich received as severe treatment as elsewhere. Felix Manz was drowned in the lake with Zwingli's approval; and in order to ensure the practice of baptism of all children the keeping of parish registers was commenced in 1526. Not the least interesting aspect of the reformation at Zurich was the spectacle of the city-state taking in hand the ordering of the religious and moral life of all its citizens. For Zwingli was not less a citizen than a preacher; and he turned to the civic organisation of the town as the natural instrument of his purposes.

Naturally the example and influence of Zurich were not without importance to other cantons of Switzerland; and from the division of the several cantons much difficulty emerged, for the effect of the Reformation was to contribute an additional element of divergence within the Confederation. Berne and Basle followed the lead of Zurich, whilst Lucerne and Freiburg adopted an independent attitude. The Roman Catholic cantons in 1524 formed a league for the suppression of heresy, looking to Ferdinand of Austria as an ally, so that Zwingli was attracted to France, whose kings combined a vigorous persecution of heresy within their own dominions with a protective assistance to Protestants in Germany and Switzerland. In 1529 war broke out between the two parties within the confederation, but was terminated in the same year by an attempted compromise by which the majority in each community of the subject territories were to decide for the old Mass or the Zwinglian *Action oder Bruch des Nachtmals*. The compromise proved unstable, and in 1531 war was renewed, and in the battle of Kappel on 11th, October 1531, Zwingli, fulfilling his civic no less than his religious duty to the last, was killed.

The divisions within the Swiss confederation produced by the Reformation were serious, but less so than the obvious threats to the Protestant movement of the disagreements upon fundamental matters of belief between Luther and Zwingli, and of the extreme opinions of the Anabaptists. The advantage presented to Rome by the divisions of its religious opponents inspired a series of conferences, notably that of Marburg in 1529, to seek a basis of agreement between the leading theologians amongst the Reformers. Between Luther and Zwingli the centre of controversy lay in their sacramental doctrines; and here the attempts at union served only to reveal the existence of irreconcilable differences. Luther, indeed, associated the Word of God closely with the Sacraments.

> In every promise of God two things are set before us, the word and the sign. The word we are to understand as being the testament, and the sign as being the sacrament; thus in the Mass the word of Christ is the testament, the bread and wine are the sacrament. And as there is greater power in the word than in the sign, so there is greater power in the testament than in the sacrament.

It followed from this that in Baptism it is not the water that produces the effects of the sacrament, " but the Word of God which accompanies and is connected with the water, and our faith, which relies on the Word of God connected with the water ". Similarly in the Mass, " the eating and drinking do not produce these great effects, but the words which stand here: ' Given and shed for you for the remission of sins ' He who believes these words has what they set forth, namely the remission of sins." In the Mass God offered to the individual believer that grace of forgiveness which is declared in the Gospel. But

Luther, whilst affirming the necessity of faith in the recipient of the Eucharist, clung tenaciously to his belief that " while both bread and wine continue there, it can be said with truth, This bread is My body; this wine is My blood, and conversely ".

Against this position of Luther, the opinions of Zwingli were equally explicit and discordant. In his judgment as expounded in his *Fidei Ratio* in 1530, " all sacraments are so far from conferring grace that they do not even bring or dispense it. . . . Sacraments are given for a public testimony of that grace which is previously present to each individual. . . . A sacrament is a sign of a sacred thing, that is, of grace which has been given."[1]

Accordingly baptism does not bring grace, but it bears witness to the Church that he to whom it is given has received grace. In like manner the Lord's Supper is " nothing else than a commemoration, whereby those who firmly believe that they have been reconciled to the Father by the death and blood of Christ announce this life-giving death, that is, praise and glory in it and proclaim it ". The presence of Christ in the Eucharist is by virtue of the remembrance on the part of the individual recipient of the benefits of Christ's life and death.[2]

Naturally Zwingli could not allow any belief such as that held by Luther (which he described as clinging to the fleshpots of Egypt) of a change in the elements of bread and wine effected by consecration. He believed that " the whole difficulty lies not in the pronoun ' this ' but in the verb ' is '. For this word is often used in Holy Scripture in the sense of ' signifies '. . . . This word ' is ' is used in this place in the sense of ' signifies '." Therefore Christ's words that the bread and wine are His body and blood are " just the same as if a wife, pointing to a ring of her hus-

---

[1] *Credo imo scio omnia sacramenta tam abesse ut gratiam conferant ut ne adferant quidem aut dispensent . . . Ex quibus hoc colligitur . . . sacramenta dari in testimonium publicum ejus gratiae, quae cuique privato prius adest . . . Credo igitur . . . sacramentum esse sacrae rei, hoe est factae gratiae, signum.*

[2] *Credo quod in Sacra Eucharistia, hoc est gratiarum actionis coena, verum Christi corpus adsit, fidei contemplatione; hoc est, quod ii qui gratias agunt Domino pro beneficio nobis in Filio suo collato, agnoscunt illum veram carnem adsumpsisse, vere in illa passum esse, vere nostra peccata sanguine suo abluisse, et sic omnem rem per Christum gestam illis fidei contemplatione velut praesentem fieri.*

band, which he had left with her, should say, 'This is my husband.'" Zwingli was at pains, against Luther, to insist that Christ's body since His ascension was in heaven, and therefore could not be present in the Eucharist. *Abiit ergo, et non est hic.* Zwingli's profoundly religious emphasis upon the necessity of preparation and faith on the part of the recipient of the Sacrament was evident in the exposition of the Order of his Communion Service appended to the *Fidei Christianae Expositio* addressed to Francis I in 1530. Nor may the importance in the Eucharist of the element of remembrance and thanksgiving for the benefits of Christ's passion—laudem et gratiarum actionem quam unigenitus Filius Dominus Noster Jesus Christus nobis ad faciendum instituit—be underestimated. But Zwingli's insistence upon this sole aspect made agreement with Luther impossible.

In his ordering of public worship Zwingli, unlike Luther and Calvin, definitely relegated the Communion to the position of a quarterly celebration, at Easter, Whitsun, Autumn and Christmas. On other Lord's Days divine service consisted of an opening prayer, the Lord's Prayer, the sermon, a confession of sins and absolution, a concluding prayer and benediction. His Order for the Communion consisted of an opening prayer, followed by a fixed Epistle (1 Cor. xi. 20–9), the *Gloria* sung antiphonally, a fixed Gospel (St. John vi. 47–62), the Nicene (or Apostles') Creed, a short admonition, the Lord's Prayer followed by further prayer, the Words of Institution, the Communion, Psalm cxiii sung antiphonally, a thanksgiving and doxology, concluding with the benediction. Luther had clung to the ideal of a weekly Communion, with sermon and communicants, a conception which was vital to Calvin. Zwingli differed from both in accepting the Holy Communion as "an occasional confessional act", to be celebrated only four times a year, though during Holy Week he commanded the young people to receive the Sacrament on Maundy Thursday, the middle-aged on Good Friday, and the old folk on Easter Day.

With his death on the field of Kappel, however, the importance of Zurich as a leader of the Reformation declined; and the centre of interest and influence removed to another Swiss

city, Geneva, which was shortly to become the scene of the
renowned labours of Calvin, for which its previous history had
provided a suitable preparation.

Historians of all shades of opinion have united in testimony
to the greatness of the work achieved by Calvin. If Luther may
claim the honour of being the founder of Protestantism, Calvin
was certainly its saviour from disruption and defeat. The
memorial of his life is writ large in Geneva particularly, but also
in other regions of Switzerland, in Germany, in France, in
Scotland, and in the Netherlands. The Anglican bishops of
Elizabethan England showed a remarkable sensitiveness to his
opinions and deference to his judgment. There is little, if any,
exaggeration in the tribute paid to his influence and authority
by the measured words of Hooker, that " of what account the
Master of the Sentences was in the Church of Rome, the same
and more amongst the preachers of the Reformed churches,
Calvin had purchased; so that the perfectest divines were judged
they which were skilfullest in Calvin's writings ". So great was
the importance of the life and work of the French Reformer
that all which has been written thus far of the history of the
Reformation might seem but the prologue to the gesta Dei
per Calvin.

Jean Cauvin, or Calvin, was born in Picardy in 1509, the son
of a lawyer, who destined him first for the priesthood and then
for the profession of the law. The young Calvin was therefore
well educated, first at Paris and also at Orléans; and from his
education he received the threefold strand which was to char-
acterise his entire life, the elements of humanism, theology, and
legal precision. His first publication was an edition of Seneca's
De Clementia, but the dominating interest of his mature mind
was to be theology, whilst from his legal training he derived a
passion for systematisation, which showed itself both in his doctrinal and practical ordering of his Church. From Picardy there
came two of the leaders of Protestantism in France, Lefèvre and
Berquin. During Calvin's youth there was indeed a considerable
movement for reform in France, where the Church stood in the
same need of purgation as in the other countries of Europe.
Jacques Lefèvre d'Etaples (Faber Stapulensis) published in 1512 a

version of the Pauline Epistles with notes, followed by the
Gospels in 1522, and by a translation of the entire Bible into
French between 1523–8. In these publications he anticipated
some of the points of Luther's theology, notably in his attack
on the mechanical interpretation of the doctrine of good works.
Amongst his pupils was Breçonnet, Abbot of St. Germain-des-
Près, who invited Lefèvre to accompany him in 1516 on his
nomination to the see of Meaux, where he was also attended
by Guillaume Farel.

Meaux became the centre of a school of reformers, emphasising the importance of faith as distinct from works, and advo-
cating the marriage of clergy and a vernacular Liturgy. They
agreed with Erasmus in desiring reform of the Church from
within, and without schism; and though Luther's writings soon
penetrated to France, they were condemned by the Sorbonne
and burned by order of the Parlement de Paris in 1521, so that
the reformers of Meaux were careful to avoid implication in the
errors of the German monk. They were protected against the
suspicions of the Sorbonne by the patronage of Margaret of
Angoulême, sister of Francis I of France. The French king
indeed was divided in policy. His rivalry with Charles V made
him lend a ready ear to proposals for alliance with the Lutheran
princes of Germany, yet he was reluctant to champion the cause
of their religious sympathisers in his own kingdom. At first he
was hesitant, appointing Lefèvre as tutor to his son, and encour-
aging the attempt of a provincial Synod at Sens to undertake
moderate reforms. The danger of reforming tendencies was
shown, however, when Farel denounced prayers for the dead,
and in 1526 Francis promised to suppress Lutheranism. The
more thoroughgoing of the French reformers therefore were
gradually driven to flight, and amongst their number was Calvin,
who in 1534 sought refuge in Basle. He had abandoned already
the career of a priest by surrendering his share in the Chapel of
Gésine and the cure of Pont L'Evêque, which had been secured
for him by his father to support him during his studies at the
university. Moreover, he had experienced a religious conversion
which ensured that henceforth his life would be devoted to the
cause of Christianity as understood by the anti-Roman reformers.

In the spring of 1536 there appeared the first edition of his *Institutes of the Christian Religion*, the book which Acton called " the finest work of Reformation literature ". In the same year he visited Geneva, and was there commanded by Farel in the name of God to share with him in the reformation of the religion and morals of that city.

The reluctant acceptance by Calvin of the command of Farel signalised the beginning of the association of Calvinism with Geneva, which has passed into history as the classic expression of the new religious system. Geneva had already embarked upon the work of reformation, in consequence of the usual combination of religious and political motives. On the one side stood its bishop, leaning for support on the Duke of Savoy, and on the other the city of Berne, anxious to extend the reformation to Geneva. The need for clerical reform was evident in Geneva, and the throwing-off of the yoke of the bishop and of Savoy would be acceptable to the civic pride of its citizens. In 1532 Farel was commissioned by Berne to labour there, and after many vicissitudes, both personal and religious, the Genevan reformation was formally confirmed in November 1535. In the following year Calvin was called to perfect the work which had been thus begun; and to his mind the profession of the Gospel involved the readiness to live according to its ethical precepts. He proposed to impose outward conformity to the beliefs and practices of the Gospel upon all citizens; and after a confused period of strife and internal dissension, both Farel and himself were driven into enforced exile in 1538. Calvin settled in Strasbourg, where Protestant and Catholic congregations lived side by side with mutual toleration, and became minister of the French refugees in that city. Here also he cemented a friendship with Bucer, played a part in the conference at Ratisbon, issued an expanded edition of his Institutes, and seemed settled in mind and estate into a fruitful vocation when the city of Geneva invited him to return. With great reluctance and only under the conviction that to decline would be to disobey a divine summons, he returned in 1540 to the city in which he was to live and work until his death in 1564.

Already the publication of two editions of his most famous

book had revealed the dominating ideas of the greatest of the Reformers. The *Christianae Religionis Institutio* of 1536 was a small volume of six chapters. Its second version of 1539 was expanded to seventeen chapters, and was translated into French in 1541. Further Latin reprints appeared in 1543, 1550, 1553, and 1554, all being duly translated into French, and the final Latin edition, further extended to four books and eighty chapters, was published in 1559, and translated into French in the following year by Calvin despite extreme illness. This book presents the core of Calvin's doctrine, both in belief and practice, and it is impossible to understand his practical work and career without reference to the principles here set out " avec rondeur et naïveté ". In style it was terse and unadorned, sacrificing every ornament to the virtues of clarity and simplicity not to say severity. Its importance in the history of Protestantism exceeded by far that of any other writings of the Reformers, for it recreated the Reformation movement and re-equipped it for defence and offence.

At the outset one of Calvin's greatest services to the cause to which his life was dedicated was the ascription of an unequivocally objective character to Protestant theology. Luther had staked all on the experience of justifying faith and upon the doctrine of *sola fides*, justification by faith alone; and his preaching had been directed entirely to the reproduction of this experience amongst his fellow-countrymen. Without doubt the grant of this justifying faith was the act of God; and equally beyond doubt it was not given as a simple matter of fact to all men. Calvin laid the foundation of his theology in the will of God, and His absolute sovereignty. God was not only the creator and ruler of the world, but the judge and lawgiver of men. Yet He is remote, inscrutable, and unapproachable by any effort which can be made on the part of sinful men. The approach must be made by God and only to those individuals whom it is His eternal purpose to save. " The Lord will have mercy upon whom He will have mercy." At the core of Calvin's theological system therefore stood the doctrine of Predestination. *Praedestinationem vocamus aeternum Dei decretum, quo apud se constitutum habuit, quid de unoquoque homine fieri vellet. Non enim pari conditione creantur*

omnes; sed aliis vita aeterna, aliis damnatio aeterna praeordinatur.[1]
The doctrine, thus stated in its simplicity and severity, sprang
from Calvin's profound sense of the transcendent and adorable
majesty of God and of the sinfulness of mankind. From before
the foundation of the world God had preordained some to salvation, others to damnation. " Israel I have loved and Esau have
I hated." Against this inscrutable and mysterious decree of God
—*decretum quidem horribile*—it was as presumptuous as profitless
to protest. It remained only to accept the fact and to educe its
implications.

Evidently only the ' elect ', that is those preordained to salvation, could possess justifying faith; for faith was not the ground
of election, but election the cause of faith. The essential basis
and principle of this doctrine of Predestination were accepted by
all the Reformers, though by none drawn out to their logical
conclusions with such thoroughness as by Calvin. It was a
necessary part of the appeal to Augustine and the revival of
Augustinianism. What was especially characteristic of Calvin
was the use which he made of the doctrine for the training or
Christian character. Luther had been much concerned with
the emotions, Zwingli with the understanding, but Calvin was
resolved to make the Church a school for the training of individual character. The conviction of election thus became not
an occasion for antinomianism or even for lethargy in ethical
behaviour, but a mainspring of positive moral conduct amongst
adherents of his Church. The persuasion of election itself was
(in the words of Article XVII of the Anglican *Articles of Religion*)
" full of sweet, pleasant, and unspeakable comfort to godly
persons, and such as feel in themselves the working of the spirit
of Christ . . . as well as because it doth greatly establish and
confirm their faith of eternal salvation to be enjoyed through
Christ, as because it doth fervently kindle their love towards
God ". To ensure the practical realisation of these ends there
was necessary a well-organised ecclesiastical society and dis-

---

[1] Predestination we call the eternal degree of God, whereby He had
determined with Himself what He willed to become of every man. For
all are not created to like estate; but to some eternal life, and to some eternal
death, is preordained.

cipline; and the originality of Calvin lay more in his polity and organisation of the Church than in his formulation of the tenets of predestination and election.

Luther indeed had early perceived that the Word of God was impotent by reason of the hardness of men's hearts to win a complete victory for the Reformation through its own inherent appeal; and accordingly had welcomed the aid of the civil power in establishing his creed, a welcome typified by the bestowal upon the chief magistrate of such high titles as *summus episcopus*, and *praecipuum membrum ecclesiae*. Zwingli had begun by making each Christian community self-governing; but the pressure of political exigency compelled him likewise to effect the work of reform at Zurich through the City Council, which was represented as acting as the delegate of the Christian communities. Calvin would have none of such expedients, and the peculiar conditions of his recall to Geneva enabled him to insist that the city which had chosen to live according to the Gospel must accept the precepts of the Church for the rule of life of its citizens. He recognised the necessity of a visible, organised church, the society of the elect, to human faith; and looking to the Epistle to the Ephesians enumerated the officers appointed by Christ in His Church, first Apostles, then Prophets, third Evangelists, fourth Pastors, and then Doctors. Of these only the two last-named were designed to be permanent, the three first being only of temporary duration. Pastors and doctors were essential to the Church: *quibus carere nunquam potest ecclesia*; and the doctors were to concern themselves with interpretation of the Scriptures, whilst the pastor's office embraced the administration of the sacraments and of discipline and the preaching of the Gospel. In other Epistles (notably in Romans xii. 7 and 1 Cor. xii. 28) St. Paul had enumerated other functions of the ministry, of which Calvin held two, those of government and the care of the poor, to be permanent. Government he interpreted as the selection of elders to administer the discipline of the Church; *gubernatores fuisse estimo seniores e plebe delectos, qui censurae morum et exercendae disciplinae una cum episcopis praeessent*: and he applied the title of bishop to those entrusted with the preaching of the Word. For the oversight of the poor, deacons were appointed. Thus Calvin furnished the Church with a four-fold ministry, of pastors, doctors, elders, and deacons; amongst which the pastors, being entrusted with the ministry of the Word, occupied a position of admitted pre-eminence. They were, ideally, to be elected with the consent and approbation of the people; and Calvin would have preferred that they should be ordained by the laying-on of hands, although this was not essential. *Licet autem nullum exstet certum praeceptum de manuum impositione, quia tamen fuisse in perpetuo usu Apostolis videmus, illa tamen accurata eorum observatio praecepti vice nobis esse debet.* Such was the doctrine of the *Institutes*.

These principles were translated into practical operation in *Les Ordonnances ecclésiastiques de l'Église de Genève* in 1541. The four-fold ministry was accepted. The pastors were to be men of proved orthodoxy of doctrine and probity of life. The rite of ordination by laying-on of hands was abandoned for the time being owing to the superstitions which had become associated with it in the past. The pastors were to hold a weekly meeting (fixed for Fridays) at which some portion of Scripture should be expounded and discussed, and attendance at this congregation was to be regarded as obligatory for the ministers of the city and of the greatest importance for those of the neighbourhood. Geneva was divided into three parishes, St. Pierre, St. Gervais, and the Madeleine; and on Sundays sermons were to be delivered in the first two of these churches at daybreak, and in all three at nine o'clock. At noon the catechising of the young was to take place, and a further sermon was to be given in each of the churches at three o'clock. On weekdays there were sermons on Monday, Wednesday, and Friday; and by the time of Calvin's death a daily sermon had been instituted in each of the city churches. To the doctors was assigned the teaching of the young, and they were to be appointed therefore by the Venerable Company (as the pastors became known). Moreover Calvin was most anxious to re-establish the College of Geneva, in order to prepare men both for civil and ecclesiastical office. The deacons, who were charged chiefly with the visitation of the sick and the relief of the poor, were likewise to be appointed by the pastors. The Elders or *Anciens* were to be a court of discipline, twelve in number, *gens de bonne vie et honeste, sans reproche et hors de toutte suspection, surtout craignans Dieu et ayans bonne prudence spirituelle.* Two were to be elected from the Little Council of the city, four from the Sixty and six from the Two Hundred, and they were to be chosen to represent every quarter of the city. Calvin had desired that the ministers should be elected by the Venerable Company alone, but the Council insisted on the prior submission of the names of all candidates for the pastor's office for its approval.

In great measure the Ordinances embodied the dominant principles of Calvin's ecclesiastical organisation. In particular the Elders were firmly established, and the meetings of the Consistory, which was composed of the ministers and the twelve ancients, presided over by one of the Syndics of the city, and assembled every Thursday, became of prime importance in the moral life of Geneva. This Consistory was predominantly a lay body, with wide powers of supervision and correction in regard to the conduct of all citizens, and expressly endowed with authority to excommunicate. In the case of offences demanding a more serious penalty than even excommunication, the offender was delivered to the Council for punishment. Around the proceedings of the Consistory great controversy centred in Calvin's lifetime in Geneva, and has continued amongst historians of his régime since his death. Its institution was essential to his system of Christian organisation. For since the city of Geneva had invited his return expressly because of their desire to adopt the precepts of the Gospel, its citizens must be taught to live according to those precepts. Some might do this of their own will and desire; but others, who would not, must be compelled. The standard of Christian conduct moreover must be determined by the Church, although the ministers were outnumbered by the laymen in the Consistory and its decisions therefore were not those of the pastors; and the decisions of the Church through the Consistory must be upheld, and where necessary enforced, by the Council. From the standpoint of the future of Protestantism the establishment of this moral discipline was of the utmost importance. Calvin thereby saved his movement from the perils of antinomianism on the one hand and of doctrinal barrenness on the other. The persuasion of election to salvation did not lead to a relaxing of moral effort nor to mere disputes upon abstruse and dark points of theological speculation. At Geneva the Gospel was not only a faith which saved but a life of intense ethical activity. With its *rectus ordo* in respect of church polity, its theological foundation firmly set forth, and its moral discipline operating through the Consistory, Calvin's church might well seem a portent to Protestant no less than to papal observers. Nor is it to be wondered that many quailed before its claims and concluded with dismay that " new presbyter is but old priest writ large ".

Notwithstanding Calvin's firm insistence upon the sovereignty of the Church, his exaltation of ecclesiastical authority implied no derogation from that of the State. To him the powers that be were truly ordained of God; and the State was entrusted by God with the responsibility of maintaining and protecting the true religion. The State must learn from the Church what is this purity of doctrine and life, but nevertheless its duty is to enforce obedience to the precepts of the Gospel. Accordingly, for Calvin the civil magistracy is a vocation of God, and of all human professions the most responsible, for in defending public morality it undertakes the protection of the standards decreed by God. From this high doctrine of the State it followed that obedience to the powers ordained of God was almost unlimited. Princes must be obeyed even though their rule was oppressive. Neither aloofness from the duties of citizenship and civil government nor rebellion against constituted authority received the approbation and countenance of Calvin. Yet for the Christian there might arise circumstances in which obedience to God must take precedence of obedience to the highest human authority. Such circumstances were restricted to the rule of a heretical or infidel sovereign, who denied the true faith and presented to his subjects the alternatives of apostasy or disobedience to his command. Rebellion could only be justified on religious grounds. For in the case of an orthodox ruler it would be his duty at the instance of the Church to put to death any teacher imperilling the salvation of the people by heretical doctrines. Thus Calvin secured the execution of Servetus, whose heresies touched the vital doctrine of the Trinity; and his attitude earned the approval of Melanchthon and Bullinger. The impossibility of limiting resistance to lawfully-constituted authority to the sole case of hostility to the true faith is evident. But Calvin looked to practical ends. He desired that his followers should be able to live at peace under Protestant princes of very varying degrees of zeal, and that under Roman Catholic sovereigns they should not lay themselves open to the charge of political rebellion. Provided the State was the defender of the true faith, its power was great; and Calvinists were able to co-operate cordially with every such State, assisting it to establish this purity of faith, doctrine, and order, and to prosecute all citizens who fell short both of its theological teaching and its ethical precepts.

In his doctrine of the sacraments, Calvin desired to steer a middle course between the theories of Luther and of Zwingli, and thereby to provide a basis for reconciliation amongst Protestants. A sacrament he defined as " an external sign, by which the Lord seals to our consciences His promises of goodwill towards us, in order to sustain the weakness of our faith; and we in turn testify our piety towards Him, as well before Himself and before angels as before men ".[1]

From this it followed that " there is never a sacrament without an antecedent promise, the sacrament being added as a kind of appendix, with a view of confirming and sealing the promise ". The Word, therefore, was indispensable to a sacrament, for it was " the promise which, proclaimed aloud by the minister, leads the people by the hand to that to which the sign tends and directs us ". Calvin insisted, in contradiction to Zwingli, that the first thing in sacraments " is that they may contribute to our faith in God, the secondary that they may attest our confession before men "; and he criticised those who made what was secondary " the first and indeed the only thing ". But faith was indispensable to the sacraments. " The office of the sacraments differs not from the Word of God: and that is, to hold forth and

---

[1] *Externum* . . . *symbolum, quo benevolentiae erga nos suae promissiones conscientiis nostris Dominus obsignat, ad sustinendam fidei nostrae imbecillitatem; et nos vicissim pietatem erga eum nostram tam coram eo et angelis quam apud homines testamur.*

offer Christ to us. . . . They confer nothing and avail nothing if not received in faith. For the sacraments are to us what messengers of good news are to men, or earnests in ratifying pactions. They do not of themselves bestow any grace, but they announce and manifest it, and, like earnests and badges, give a ratification of the gifts which the Divine liberality has bestowed upon us." Thus, although Calvin parted from Zwingli, he repudiated the traditional Catholic doctrine with equal emphasis. He drew a parallel between the sacraments of the Old Testament and the New, with only this difference, " that while the former shadowed forth a promised Christ while He was still expected, the latter bear testimony to Him as already come and manifested ". Despite the efficacy of sacraments, the Word retained its position of superiority. For " the assurance of salvation does not depend on participation in the sacraments, as if justification consisted in it. This, which is treasured up in Christ alone, we know to be communicated, not less by the preaching of the Gospel than by the seal of a sacrament, and may be completely enjoyed without this seal."

This was the doctrine of the Institutes: *De Sacramentis*. Applying these general principles to particular sacramental rites, Calvin considered Baptism as " the initiatory sign by which we are admitted to the fellowship of the Church, that being ingrafted into Christ, we may be accounted children of God ". The Eucharist is " a pledge to assure us of God's continued liberality ", and " the chief and almost the whole energy of the sacrament consists in these words: ' It is broken for you: it is shed for you.' It would not be of much importance to us that the body and blood of the Lord are now distributed had they not once been set forth for our redemption and salvation." In treating of the vital question of the nature of the presence of Christ in the Supper, Calvin did not attempt a clear-cut definition of the mystery. *Quodsi verum est praeberi nobis signum visibile ad obsignandam invisibilis rei donationem, accepto corporis symbolo, non minus corpus etiam ipsum nobis dari certo confidamus.* He would not allow the idea that " to eat the flesh of Christ is no other than to believe in Christ Himself ", and equally he repudiated the belief in the transformation of the elements of bread and wine by consecration into the body and blood of Christ. In the Institutes he affirmed, *dico igitur in Coenae mysterio per symbola panis et vini Christum vere nobis exhibere adeoque corpus et sanguinem ejus.* But he found no inconsistency in accepting the mystery without explanation. " If any one enquire of me respecting the manner, I shall not be ashamed to acknowledge that it is a mystery too sublime for me to be able to express, or even to comprehend. . . . I rather experience than understand it." Similarly in *La Petite Traicté de la Cène*, written in 1542, he declared:

> We acknowledge therefore that by receiving with faith the Sacrament according to the ordinance of the Lord, we are truly made partakers of the very substance of the body and blood of Jesus Christ. How this comes to pass, some can declare and explain more clearly than others. On the one hand, in order to exclude all carnal imaginations, we must lift up our hearts to heaven, not supposing that our Lord Jesus could so descend as to be enclosed within corruptible elements. On the other hand, in order not to diminish the efficacy of this holy mystery, we must believe that it is effected by the secret and miraculous power of God, and that the Spirit of God is the means of our partaking, which is therefore said to be a spiritual partaking.

In the celebration of the Lord's Supper Calvin agreed with Zwingli against Luther in abolishing ceremonies reminiscent of the Roman Mass and making Scripture alone the test of what should be included. His Order for the Communion, to be conducted at the Holy Table, began with a confession of sin, a form of absolution, and a psalm; and then the minister proceeded to the pulpit. There he uttered a prayer, read the Scripture lesson, preached the sermon in exposition thereof, and returned to the Holy Table for the Communion. A prayer of intercession followed, with the Lord's Prayer, the Apostles' Creed, the central prayer, including the Words of Institution and exhortation and excommunication of the unworthy, the Communion, an admonition to lift up the heart to the ascended Christ, a hymn, thanksgiving, Nunc Dimittis, and benediction. Upon the frequent celebration of the Communion (accompanied by the singing of metrical psalms, those *psaumes français* as characteristic of the Reformed churches as the Lutheran hymns of its churches) Calvin laid much stress as the core of the Reformed public worship. In the Institutes and elsewhere he expressed his lifelong conviction that the Communion should be celebrated " very frequently, and at least once in every week ", *singulis ad minimum hebdomadibus*; and in the Ordinances which he drew up for Geneva he prescribed its celebration once each month in the churches of the city itself, and quarterly in every parish. On this point, however, he had to give way to the determination of the Council, which ruled that for the present the Lord's Supper should be celebrated only four times per year, at Christmas, Easter, Whitsun, and the first Sunday in September. On other Sundays the Reformed Service was truncated to the traditional Ante-Communion. Thus at Geneva, as elsewhere, the laudable intention of the Reformers to turn the Mass into a Communion and therewith to restore the apostolic custom of its administration every Lord's Day was frustrated by the conservatism of the laity, who refused so great an advance on their tradition of annual reception and accepted only the compromise of a quarterly Communion.

Calvin's work at Geneva had both a local and an œcumenical aspect. Locally the circumstances of the city and of its renowned leader were unique. Situated almost on the borders of the French kingdom, Geneva became a city of refuge for Protestants not only from France but from many other European countries including England and Italy. Yet Calvin was not admitted to its citizenship until he had rendered eighteen years of service to its church. Himself an exile from his own country with no hopes of return or patronage from its rulers, he was not limited, as was Luther, by the political necessity of compromise in order to win the support of civil princes, but was freed to work out the pattern of a true Scriptural church directing the life of a Christian community. Moreover, the conditions of his recall to Geneva gave him peculiar authority to carry out his will, modelling its constitution after the principles of a theocracy, in which the church proclaimed true doctrine and the law of Christian conduct, and the civil power lent its sanctions to the ecclesiastical discipline. Thus Geneva became in the eyes of its disciples as a city set upon a hill, whose light was set for the leading of the nations.

Its influence, however, was not to be limited to the witness of silent example. Not the least important of the achievements of

Calvin was his establishment of the University of Geneva, a project which had been foremost in his thoughts from the beginning of his work there. Geneva was to be not merely a pattern of a true Scriptural church and community but a missionary centre from which there should proceed evangelists, equipped and trained to propagate the doctrine and practice of Calvin's system. To this end there was need of an academy which should possess towards the churches of the Protestant movement a similar authority to that of the University of Paris in the Roman Catholic world. In 1556 Calvin laid before the Council of Geneva his scheme for the reorganisation of public instruction; and, although the progress of the work was hindered by various difficulties, the new Collège de Genève was inaugurated in 1559, though the building itself was not completed until 1564. This great work of education and propaganda was financed by public and private donations; and by a singular stroke of good fortune for Calvin, a dispute between the ministers and college at Lausanne and the Council of that city led to the emigration of all the professoriate to Geneva in 1559, there to become teachers in his new foundation. Beza was the first Rector of the University at Geneva; and the success of the experiment was such that, beginning with 162 pupils in its first year, by the time of Calvin's death in 1564 its numbers had risen to 1500, of whom the greater part were foreigners. Thus the Geneva Academy became the seminary of the Protestant Reformed movement throughout Europe, sending forth zealous ministers, many of whom were Calvin's fellow-countrymen and took their lives in their hands in returning to their native land. The foundation of this academy indeed set the seal upon Calvin's work at Geneva.

In other respects also he became a figure of international influence. His especial concern was for the healing of the divisions amongst Swiss Protestants as a first step towards agreement between all Protestant churches against their common enemy, Rome. After intermittent negotiations conducted by correspondence with Bullinger of Zurich, a personal meeting between himself, Farel, and Bullinger in 1549 led to the conclusion of the *Consensus Tigurinus*, in which the conception of sacraments as *signa nuda* was formally abandoned and Zurich accepted Calvin's sacramental doctrine as the standard of belief. This agreement was accepted at once by St. Gall, Schaffhausen, and Neufchatel, and Berne and Basle signified their assent after an interval. Thus the Consensus became the basis of the Second Helvetic Confession of 1566 by which the religious unity of the Swiss Protestants was finally and formally sealed. It was the progenitor also of similar agreements in other parts of Europe, such as the Heidelberg Catechism of 1563, and the Confessio Czengerina of 1557 of the Magyar majority of the Reformation bodies in Hungary. Unfortunately it frustrated the hope of agreement with the Lutheran churches of Germany, which were falling into increasing divisions, and which had made no provision in the peace of Augsburg of 1555 for the toleration of the Reformed churches, an omission fatal to its success as a solution of the religious divisions of the Empire. Thus Calvinists and Lutherans continued divided from each other, a condition which led to such curious circumstances as the inability of any Lutheran to become a citizen of Geneva or of any Calvinist to become a citizen of Hamburg. More serious was the obstacle thereby set up to Calvin's cherished dream of a General Council of all Protestant churches to frame an agreed doctrinal confession and to achieve a unity of policy in face of the growing menace of Rome, awakened at length to the extent and gravity of the schism produced by the Reformation movement. This hope was not to be realised; for the nearest approach to its expression was seen half a century after Calvin's death in the Synod of Dort in 1618–19, to which there came representatives from all the Dutch States, from Switzerland, from the churches of the Palatinate, Hesse, Nassau, Bremen, from Scotland, and from the episcopal Church of England, whilst Louis XIII refused permission to the French delegates to leave their country. Notwithstanding the evident inadequacy of this synod to attain the character of Protestant œcumenicity, its summons and the diversity of countries represented at its sessions were evidence of the international penetration of the Reformed churches.

Calvin's interest and sympathy were naturally concerned closely in the fortunes of Protestantism in his native France. There Protestantism never became more than the religion of a minority, not only because of the strength of the monarchy and its hostility to the Reformation within its own kingdom but also because France was predominantly a rural country and the great majority of the peasantry never wavered from their traditional faith. The minority, however, which was sympathetic towards the Reformed doctrines was influential. Persecution during the reigns of Francis I and Henry II, though severe at times, was intermittent, owing to the preoccupation of the kings with their political rivalry with the Habsburg house and their military campaigns in Italy. Meanwhile little groups of *fidèles* assembled in secret for prayer and the study of the Bible, and incipient congregations were created in the capital and the chief towns, encouraged by a stream of *colporteurs* from Geneva. Many difficulties lay at first in the way of the provision of ministers, and the faithful had to rely chiefly on the services of itinerant ministers, whilst building up a voluntary organisation of deacons and elders according to the Genevan model. In 1555 the first Evangelical Church of Paris was established with a settled minister, and other towns followed this example with such success that in 1559 when the first National Synod of the French Reformed Church met in the capital, no fewer than seventy-two local churches were represented. After the foundation of the university of Geneva the provision of a supply of ministers was ensured, so that nineteen ministers came to France in 1559, twelve in 1560, and ninety in 1561. The National Synod adopted a confession of faith, the *Confessio Gallicana*, drawn up largely according to a draft sent by Calvin himself, and a scheme of organisation, *La Discipline Ecclèsiastique*. This scheme adapted the principles of Geneva to the very different conditions of a series of scattered congregations, forming part of a powerful national State, and endeavoured to strike the mean between too complete an independence of each local congregation and too great super-vision by a national synod. Each local church was to have its own consistory, but no church nor minister was to claim any authority over any other church or minister. From each local church there were to come to the national synod the minister with not more than one or two elders or deacons. In regard to the authorisation of ministers, the rite of presbyteral ordination by imposition of hands was prescribed *toutefois sans aucune super-stition*, and ordination so given was to constitute a life-commission, not a mere temporary function.

Meanwhile a new element entered into the history of the French Reformed Church by the adherence of some of the leading noble families, who introduced a political character to what had hitherto been a religious movement. Thus the fortunes of the Huguenot cause became inextricably involved with the family and political rivalries of France, from which there ensued the dismal generation of wars of religion, the mediating and often vacillating policy of Catherine de Medicis, the dramatic episode of the massacre on St. Bartholomew's Day, 1572, the rivalry of the Guise family and Henry of Navarre, and the final victory of the latter accompanied by his conversion to Roman Catholicism. With the end of the protracted and dreary wars of religion, the Huguenots received their reward in the Edict of Nantes of 1598. An early attempt at theological agreement between Huguenots and Roman Catholics at the Colloquy of Poissey in 1561 had demonstrated the impossibility of compromise; and by the Edict of Nantes the former received religious toleration, the promise of civil equality, and the provision of garrisoned fortresses as a protection of their liberties. Although the terms of this settlement were more tolerant and liberal than any known to Europe for more than a century afterwards, the French Reformed churches remained conscious of their continuing position as a minority of the nation, of which their military privileges were a symbol. Equally symbolical of their inferiority was the prohibition of Protestant worship in Paris, so that the faithful Huguenots of the capital had to repair by barge to Charenton. Notwithstanding such restrictions and the withdrawal of the military concessions by Richelieu, the reigns of Henri IV and, to a lesser degree, of Louis XIII constituted a comparative golden age for French Protestants, and they remained in enjoyment of their religious liberties until the revocation of the edict in 1685 by Louis XIV. Calvin was not left, therefore, without witness in the land of his birth, though in France Calvinism never approached the position of the religion of the majority of the people.

Into the Empire the Reformed Church entered as a further dividing force. With the increasing divisions within the Lutheran churches after the death of Luther, and as a result of its own superior theological and administrative position, Calvinism displaced Lutheranism as the protagonist of Protestantism. Along the valley of the Rhine, especially in the Palatinate, it secured a firm establishment; and the exclusion from the peace of Augsburg of any provision for the Reformed system was a contributory cause of the Thirty Years' War which devastated Germany from 1618 to 1648, in which Denmark, Sweden, and France all played their part in the saving of Protestantism and the ruin of Germany. Farther east, Ferdinand II allowed little opportunity for the Reformed faith to take root in Austria and Styria, but in Hungary and its dependencies, which were largely subject to Turkish suzerainty, both Lutheran and Calvinist churches were established, the former being largely confined to the German peoples and the latter taking firm hold upon the Magyars.

In another part of the Empire, the Netherlands, a further act of the drama of Calvinism was to be played amid singularly confused circumstances. Ecclesiastically the greater part of their territory lay in the dioceses of Tournai, Arras, and Utrecht (the last see together with that of Liége being important immediate bishoprics), but part lay also within the sees of Térouenne, Cambrai, and Liége. Moreover, the controlling archbishops belonged to foreign countries, so that conditions were favourable for the spread of Reforming doctrines, since the ecclesiastical administration was characterised by great confusion. So early as 1521 Charles V issued an edict against Lutheranism, for Lutheran writings had made their appearance already in the Netherlands. In 1527 the diocese of Utrecht was so troubled by Protestantism, which its bishop found beyond his powers to control, that Charles secured the surrender to himself of its temporal lordship in return for his promise to stamp out heresy. Despite the introduction of the Inquisition into the Netherlands, the effective suppression of Protestantism was impossible in the great towns. When Charles abdicated after the peace of Augsburg in 1555, leaving Philip II to grapple with the problems of the Netherlands, the situation became rapidly acute. In 1557 the new sovereign proposed the foundation and endowment from monastic revenues of fourteen new bishoprics with three archbishoprics, but this extensive measure of ecclesiastical reform provoked great opposition on the ground of its supposed favouring of the interests of Spain. Consequently the struggle for religious freedom became involved with that for national independence of Spanish influence. The Protestant movement, however, was divided within itself, Lutheran, Calvinist, and Anabaptist elements being present in involuntary juxtaposition; and moreover the violence of some Reformers, seen in the iconoclastic riots of 1566, alienated many moderate and conservative Roman Catholics. Thus the southern provinces separated from the northern, preferring to make what terms they could with Philip than to go forward in the company of Protestant extremists. The northern states under the leadership of William the Silent formed the Union of Utrecht, which finally carried their cause to actual victory in 1609, though the formal international recognition of their independence was not achieved until the peace of Westphalia in 1648.

Within the United Provinces, which thus asserted their independence of foreign rule, Calvinism was the superior creed, though Lutherans and Anabaptists were allowed freedom of conscience though not of proselytising. In its organisation in the Netherlands Calvinism reproduced the sturdy emphasis upon the independence of the church which had characterised its establishment in Geneva. In the *Confessio Belgica* of 1561 the discipline of the church for the punishment of sin, its authority to excommunicate, and the duty of the civil power to protect and defend the church in its disciplinary system, were clearly laid down. Accordingly the Reformed system fashioned itself after the theocratic model of Geneva, and in the foundation of the university of Leyden in 1575 possessed an intellectual centre comparable to the academy of Calvin's establishment. Leyden indeed was distinguished by three scholars of European eminence, in Scaliger, Grotius, and Arminius, although the last-named was associated with a theological position which challenged the fundamental tenets of Calvin concerning predestination and the freedom of the will. Nowhere amid the countries of Europe did the Reformed faith and polity establish itself more firmly than in the United Provinces.

Yet the Netherlands, like the Swiss cantons, were too small in territorial extent and possessed of too strong a tradition of civic independence to form a suitable ground for the adaptation of the Calvinistic system to the religious organisation of an entire kingdom. In some aspects the fullest realisation of the ideals of Calvin was achieved in Scotland. There the old régime was disfigured by greater abuses than perhaps in any other European country, and provided a promising field for the most thorough-going reformation. In Scotland, too, the first stirrings of revolt took the form of the dissemination of Lutheran opinions, and there also Calvinism swept its rival from the field no less completely than it did their common enemy, the papal authority. The Reformation was inevitably associated with political factors, and attained a good degree of popularity, especially amongst the nobility, by its opposition to the foreign domination of France through the hated Guise family. The religious leader of the Scottish Reformation was John Knox, himself a disciple of an earlier reformer, George Wishart, and a fervent disciple also of Calvin. In 1559 Knox's return to Scotland was the signal for an outbreak of iconoclasm and rebellion, which resulted in the abolition by authority of the Scottish parliament of the papal jurisdiction and of the Mass, and the adoption of a Confession of Faith, and of the First Book of Discipline in the following year. Based upon the doctrine of Calvin, the Confession possessed a plainness and vigour of speech typical of the exacerbation of contemporary strife in its denunciation of that " filthie synagogue " and " horrible harlot, the Kirk malignant ". It remained the standard of belief in the Church of Scotland until the promulgation in 1647 of the Westminster Confession. The Book of Discipline adopted Calvin's fourfold ministry, but provided for an authorised deviation from the strict principle of the parity of ministers by allowing the institution of Superintendents, upon which basis the Stuart kings later tried to reintroduce episcopacy. It insisted upon popular nomination of ministers, and refused to allow any to be a minister save a preacher, for even the Sacraments cannot be " rightlie ministred by him in whose mouth God hath put no sermon of exhortation ". As at Geneva, so in Scotland the Reformed Church showed great zeal for education, since upon the right understanding of Scripture depended much of the good estate of the faithful. In 1564 the General Assembly accepted the Book of Common Order which followed the form of public worship drawn up by Calvin at Geneva. After Knox's death a second confession of faith and book of discipline were issued, which allowed presbyteral ordination by imposition of hands, and fulminated against the decrees of the Council of Trent.

Thus in Scotland the Reformed system entered into its full heritage as a national established church. Its ministers inherited the parochial system and churches of the old régime, establishing there the consistory, and the local churches were linked together in a national synod, the General Assembly. Thus instead of the small extent of the city-state of Geneva, in Scotland an entire people were moulded into a godly commonwealth. Nor was the desire lacking to extend the example to England, and, by abolishing the Royal Supremacy, the episcopate, the Book of Common Prayer, to unite Great Britain into an evangelical nation. This hope was not destined to be realised. But through Scotland, France, the Netherlands, the Rhineland, Switzerland, Hungary, and Poland stretched a belt of Reformed churches, enclosing the Lutheran establishments of the Empire and the Scandinavian countries, and constituting the strongest line of defence of Protestantism against the revived energy of Rome. Such were the fruits of Calvin's life and work, and such the inspiration of Geneva where he had established, according to the judgment of Knox, " the most perfect school of Christ that ever was on earth since the days of the Apostles ".

CHAPTER IV

ANGLICANISM AND THE REFORMATION IN ENGLAND

THE general condition of the *Ecclesia Anglicana* on the eve
of the Reformation was similar to that of the Church in
France and the Empire, presenting ample ground for the de-
nouncer of abuses and prophet of reform. The episcopate, as
has been already observed, was recruited chiefly from the ranks
of clergy experienced in diplomacy and political administration,
and one of its gravest weaknesses in face of new critical tendencies
was the lack of theologians amongst its personnel. The consequent neglect of pastoral oversight on the part of the bishops
led to widespread laxity amongst the inferior clergy. The higher
clergy associated with the cathedral and collegiate churches were
infected by the prevalent worldliness, whilst the parochial
system had suffered so many inroads from appropriations, dispensations from residence, pluralism, and the resultant poverty
of those priests entrusted with the pastoral care, as to stand in
need of thoroughgoing reform. The monastic houses generally
were weakened by lack of vocations, laxity in the observance
of rule, and financial mismanagement, which called for a considerable redistribution of revenues and personnel. Moreover,
there was much vigorous criticism among classes able to make
vocal their discontent with the entire hierarchy of ecclesiastical
courts from the archiepiscopal down to the archidiaconal, on
the ground of excessive charges, dilatory procedure, and rapacity
in seeking to extend their jurisdiction. The hostility of the faithful Commons of Henry VIII's parliament of 1529–36 to the ecclesiastical administration was one of the most noteworthy features
of its legislation. The Papacy likewise was felt in England chiefly
in its capacity of tax-collector, for England had borne the loyal
character of " the milch cow of the Papacy " at the height of
the Middle Ages.

Nor was the dissatisfaction confined to financial and judicial matters. Evidence survives of the existence of subterranean currents of discontent and criticism of doctrinal subjects, though it is almost impossible to ascertain the extent of such movements of opinion. Lollardy had never been entirely suppressed, for at intervals throughout the reign of Henry VII there were executions for heresy. There seems, indeed, to have been a recrudescence of such tendencies towards the end of his reign and the beginning of that of his son, for Archbishop Warham summoned a Convocation in 1512 to deal with the question of repression of heresy, which, though it did not get far in fulfilment of its aim, heard the famous sermon of John Colet in denunciation of ecclesiastical abuses from the highest to the lowest ranks of the clergy. When evidences of Lutheran opinions appeared in England, they were regarded at first as further cells of Lollardy. Nor did echoes of events in the Empire tarry in reaching this country. Trade connections with the Netherlands brought Lutheran opinions especially to Norfolk, whilst Lutheran literature was smuggled through the Steelyard in London. Luther's popular writings of 1520 found a very early entry into England, and in 1521 Henry VIII earned the gratitude of the Papacy and the title of *Fidei Defensor* by his refutation of the German reformer's sacramental errors. In 1526 also there came into the country copies of Tyndale's New Testament in English, smuggled from the Continent. Such movements of criticism were reinforced, albeit involuntarily, by the strictures of the school of Oxford reformers, amongst which Colet and Erasmus are numbered. This school desired a purgation of the Church by educational reform and without schism. In 1497 Colet began at Oxford his continuous exposition of St. Paul's Epistles, in which he endeavoured to ascertain their grammatical and literal meaning, laying aside allegorical and scholastic interpretations. He neither advocated revolt nor demanded any breach with Rome; yet to his position the office of the Papacy was not essential to the Church. More famous was the cosmopolitan scholar, Erasmus, the bitter satirist of monks and scholasticism, but also the constructive writer whose editions of the New Testament in Greek, and of the Greek patristic writings, established his influence widely, and in circles with which he had little sympathy in respect of the use which they made of his learning. Moreover, in England, as on the Continent, some of the actual leaders of the Reformation were themselves regular clergy, who had imbibed the principles of revolt within monastic houses, as was the case with John Whitgift, afterwards Archbishop of Canterbury, who was taught by his uncle Robert, abbot of Wellow, a house of Black Augustinian Canons, near Grimsby. In monasteries and in the universities, as in the Cambridge circle from which proceeded Cranmer, Coverdale, Tyndale, and Latimer, earnest students, discontented with the established ecclesiastical system, were occupying themselves by reading of the Bible and of Luther's works in the quest for a new and more satisfying scheme of faith and practice.

There were many tendencies in the England to which Henry VIII succeeded as undisputed king in 1509 which had prepared the ground for a reform of the Church both in organisation and doctrine. From none of these sources, however, was the actual impulse which provoked the Anglican Reformation to come. Its occasion was the episode of Henry VIII's desire to ensure a legitimate male heir to his throne, and as a means to this end to put away Catherine of Aragon, his brother's widow and subsequently his own wife, in favour of Anne Boleyn. The incident has been well advertised and is perhaps the best-known feature of Henry VIII's life and times. Nor is it difficult to perceive that from the miserable story of the " divorce " the only actor emerging with dignity and credit was Catherine herself. But the episode was the occasion of the Reformation, not its cause; and regarded solely as a matrimonial question it must be set alongside other contemporary marriage alliances of an epoch singularly characterised by irregularity and infidelity. An investigation of the marriage customs of royal and noble houses in fifteenth- and sixteenth-century Europe would be as unedifying as unprofitable, from which neither popes nor sovereigns would emerge with a certificate of honour. Henry VIII was not alone in his desire to get rid of one wife and espouse another; and if Catherine had been willing, as was Jean, the wife of Louis XII of France, to embrace the religious vocation, no difficulties would have ensued for the English king. Nor is it possible to separate the attitude of Pope Clement VII towards Henry's problem from the political exigencies of his situation, especially after the capture and sack of Rome in 1527 and his consequent position as the virtual prisoner of Charles V, the nephew of Catherine. In view, however, of the accidental character of the marriage question as only the immediate occasion of the English breach with Rome, it is unnecessary to dwell further upon its protracted history.

The summons of Parliament in 1529 in such circumstances marked the beginning of a new epoch in English history. Its initial act was the presentation of a detailed complaint of ecclesiastical abuses; whilst in the Convocation the whole estate of the clergy was held by its recognition of Wolsey's legatine authority to have fallen under the penalties of praemunire. The price of the royal pardon was to be heavy; a large money subsidy and a declaration in respect of the Crown that " of the church and clergy of England, whose especial Protector and single, supreme lord, and, as far as the law of Christ allows, even Supreme Head, we acknowledge His Majesty to be ". The threat to the clerical order presented by the hostile attitude of the Commons led to the Submission of the Clergy, by which they tried to secure the protection of the sovereign against their adversaries. To this end the Convocation accepted severe restrictions upon its power; by consenting that its meeting must be in response to a summons of the king sent to the archbishop, that no new canons should be made without royal licence and assent, and that the existing Canon Law should be committed to examination by a commission of thirty-two, half of whom should be laity. The way was now free for Henry to effect his will through the agency of Parliament, which proceeded to enact a series of statutes severing the financial and judicial connection with Rome, prescribing methods for the transaction of all ecclesiastical administration within the realm, and culminating in the declaration of the Royal Supremacy. Thus the Church of England was removed from the jurisdiction and authority of the Papacy.

Meanwhile the See of Canterbury, falling vacant by the death of Warham in 1532, had been filled with the most scrupulous care for the external conditions of validity, by the appointment of Thomas Cranmer in accordance with papal approval. Cranmer proceeded to determine 'the king's privy matter' in his archiepiscopal court, pronouncing the marriage with Catherine invalid, and preparing the way for the legitimisation of Henry's marriage with Anne Boleyn (which had already taken place secretly) and of the birth of the Princess Elizabeth. The king had acted throughout with great regard for the external appearances of legality. Moreover, his acts had been professedly based upon a constant appeal to history in support of his claim to be resuming to the crown its traditional and rightful privileges, which had been usurped by the Bishop of Rome. The famous preamble to the Act of Appeals of 1533 declared that

> by divers sundry old authentic histories and chronicles it is manifestly declared and expressed that this realm of England is an empire, and so hath been accepted in the world, governed by one supreme head and king . . . unto whom a body politic, compact of all sorts and degrees of people divided in terms and by names of spiritualty and temporalty, be bounden and ought to bear, next to God, a natural and humble obedience.

Similarly the Act of Supremacy did not profess to be creating any new title or position for the king, but only required him to " be taken, accepted, and reputed the only supreme head in earth of the Church of England, called *Anglicana Ecclesia* ". The principle of the Henrician reformation was the assertion of the sovereignty of the national kingdom alike in matters ecclesiastical and civil. At the same time, these very statutes reiterated the theological orthodoxy of king and church in England. The Act for the conditional restraint of Annates in 1532 affirmed that the king's subjects were " as devout, obedient, catholic, and humble children of God and Holy Church as any people be within any realm christened "; and the Act forbidding papal dispensations and payment of Peter's pence in 1534 insisted that the Church of England had no design " to decline or vary from the congregation of Christ's Church in any things concerning the very articles of the Catholic Faith of Christendom, or in any other things declared by Holy Scripture and the Word of God, necessary for your and their salvation ". Not without reason has Henry VIII's reformation been described as Catholicism without the Papacy.

The legislative programme was followed by the suppression of all monasteries and religious orders, their estates being confiscated by the crown, and only five new bishoprics being established permanently out of their revenues. Perhaps the most remarkable feature of the suppression was the high proportion of regulars who accepted the new order and office within it. This is characteristic also of the great majority of the secular clergy. The martyrs for the Papacy were few in number, though some of them were eminent in position and character, such as Bishop Fisher of Rochester, Sir Thomas More, and the Carthusians of London. Notwithstanding these illustrious exceptions, the fact remains and challenges explanation that they were exceptional, whereas the vast majority of clergy, secular and regular, not only accepted the changes but retained office throughout the even greater changes of the succeeding reign. Moreover, the intellectual respectability of Henry's reformation was established by the defence put forth by so learned and conservative a bishop as Gardiner in his *De Vera Obedientia Oratio*. For the majority of clergy to whom such intellectual considerations made little appeal, the old system was not sufficiently a matter of conviction to justify resignation of their cures. Perhaps the severest criticism of the old order is that revealed in the twin circumstances that prelates such as Gardiner could believe the Papacy unessential to the Catholic Church and so high a proportion of the clergy regard its repudiation with indifference. The continuance in office of so many clergy proved an important barrier to the spread of reformed opinions, as Bishop Hooper of Gloucester found at a later date to his chagrin.

The presence upon the episcopal bench, however, of divines of known reforming sympathies, such as Latimer of Worcester, Shaxton of Sarum, and Foxe of Hereford, especially with Cranmer at Canterbury, raised doubts as to the possibility of stopping short at the administrative changes effected by the Reformation parliament. The Lower House of Convocation in 1536 presented sixty-seven *mala dogmata* which they affirmed to be current, and which embraced such typical features of Protestant opinions as disrespect for the Mass, questioning the authority of the priesthood, demanding the Communion in both kinds, and criticism of the honours paid to the Blessed Virgin Mary and the saints. In the same year a Book of Ten Articles was drawn up by the bishops to define the standpoint of the Church of England, and its attitude was markedly conservative. The rule of faith was declared to be the Scriptures, the three Creeds, the authority of the Fathers, and the first four General Councils. The Sacraments were not enumerated, and only three were defined. The doctrine of Transubstantiation was accepted, the sacrament of penance regarded as of divine institution and as necessary for salvation, the saints were to be honoured and even prayed to, the veneration of images was declared to be excellent and a means of raising the soul to things beyond the senses, justification was asserted but not defined, prayers and even Masses for the departed were commanded, and traditional ceremonies were to be retained. Here was little promise of rapid or thoroughgoing reformation. Nor did the further doctrinal definitions of the reign of Henry VIII belie this anticipation. *The Godly and Pious Institution of a Christian Man* of 1537 was an orthodox exposition of the Creed, the seven Sacraments, the Ten Commandments, the Pater Noster and Ave Maria, and of justification and prayers for the dead; whilst the VI Articles Act of 1539 was a declaration of rigid orthodoxy. Transubstantiation was affirmed, communion in both kinds was declared not to be necessary to salvation, priests were forbidden to marry, vows of chastity once taken were binding, private Masses were to be continued and were agreeable to God's law, and auricular confession was necessary and to be retained. The penalties for disobedience were heavy, and if the Act had been rigorously enforced, the results would have been grave. Its passing provoked the resignation of Latimer and Shaxton, whilst Cranmer put away his wife. In 1543 the issue of *A Necessary Doctrine and Erudition for a Christian Man* followed the general lines of the preceding volume of 1537.

If signs of advance towards reformed doctrine were to be found, they were not so emphatic or direct as the affirmations of substantial orthodoxy. In 1536 there were issued the first Royal Injunctions of Henry VIII by which the clergy were required to explain to their people the Ten Articles, to confine their teaching concerning relics, images, and saints to the provisions of these articles, and to teach the Creed, the Commandments, and the Pater Noster in the vulgar tongue. In 1538 there appeared the second Royal Injunctions, which required the setting up in every parish church of " one book of the whole Bible of the largest volume in English " for reading by the people. The clergy were to encourage their flock " to read the same, as that which is the very lively word of God, that every Christian man is bound to embrace, believe, and follow if he look to be saved ". Likewise the clergy were to enquire of their people at their resort to confession in Lent whether they could say the Apostles' Creed and the Pater Noster in English, declaring " that every Christian person ought to know the same before they should receive the blessed Sacrament of the altar ". Every quarter at least the clergy should preach one sermon setting forth " the very gospel of Christ ", and discouraging pilgrimages, the burning of candles before images or relics, and kissing the same; to which end no lights should be burned before any image or relic, leaving only " the light that commonly goeth across the church by the rood-loft, the light before the Sacrament of the altar, and the light about the sepulchre ". Moreover, incumbents were to recant their former erroneous teaching concerning pilgrimages, relics, and images, declaring that they " did the same upon no ground of Scripture ". These injunctions were attended by a whole-sale destruction of famous shrines, such as those of our Lady at Ipswich and Walsingham, and that of Becket at Canterbury, and of famous images such as the rood of Boxley; whereby some of the most popular signs of the traditional system were abolished. Political considerations mingled with religious in such iconoclasm, but the effect upon the unlettered population was not without importance.

It cannot be doubted, however, that the most influential of all the items of the Injunctions was that requiring the setting up in every church of the Great Bible. This step, together with the command that clergy should admonish their " parishioners that images serve for none other purpose but as to be books of unlearned men that cannot know letters, whereby they might be otherwise admonished of the lives and conversation of them that the said images do represent ", may not unfairly be said to have laid the axe to the root of the tree, though the complete fall of the old system was yet to be effected. The importance of the vernacular Bible was as great in England as in Germany, perhaps even greater, for the English Reformation gave birth to no such outburst of hymnody as the Lutheran movement. The setting up of the Great Bible had been preceded by Tyndale's New Testament in 1526, and by the English Bible of Coverdale in 1535, and that of Matthew in 1537; but whereas the hand of authority had been invoked against previous attempts at popular circulation, the second Injunctions of Henry VIII approved the installation and reading of the vernacular Scriptures. The influence of this step on the official formularies of the Church of England may be seen in the Ordinal and the Articles of Religion of the reign of Edward VI. But beyond its importance in this connection, the popularisation of the English Bible led to that silent religious revolution which produced a new pattern of individual and family piety and found public expression throughout the history of seventeenth-century England. For the moment, however, it was in advance of the main position of royal policy in religion, and it was followed only by the issue in 1545 from the hand of Cranmer of an English Litany for public use, and by the publication of a Primer of English prayers for private use, bearing the name and authorisation of the king. When Henry VIII died in 1547 the Reformation in England was in a state of suspended development.

During the short reign of his son Edward VI its development proceeded with equal rapidity and rapacity on the part of the young king's regents. The five years from 1547 to 1552 saw the publication of the First and Second Prayer Books of Edward VI, of the Ordinal, and of a Confession of Faith in the form of the Forty-Two Articles of Religion, as well as an Act of Parliament permitting clerical marriages, and further iconoclastic episodes. With the accession of Mary Tudor in 1553 a complete reaction ensued, expressed in the repeal of all legislation concerning the Church both of Edward VI and of Henry VIII, and culminating in the restoration of the papal supremacy; during the course of which process many of the leaders of the Reformation, including

Cranmer himself, perished, whilst less bold spirits found refuge abroad, notably in Frankfurt and Geneva. On the accession of Elizabeth in 1558 the pendulum swung back again. The papal obedience was repudiated, the statutes of Henry VIII revived (the Queen substituting for the title 'Supreme Head' that of 'Supreme Governor'), a modified version of the second Edwardine Prayer Book authorised, the Articles of Religion reduced to Thirty-Nine, and the episcopate replenished from the ranks of the returned exiles. With the establishment of Elizabeth's religious settlement, the Church of England settled down to the task of developing and expounding its theological and ecclesiastical position.

The Prayer Books were chiefly the work of Cranmer, whose liturgical studies had led him to consult Eastern as well as Roman rites and to compare both with contemporary experiments in his endeavour to frame a vernacular English Liturgy. The Mass of the 1549 book embraced the Lord's Prayer, Collect for Purity, Introit, ninefold Kyrie, Gloria in excelsis, Collect, Epistle and Gospel, Nicene Creed, Sermon, Sursum Corda, Preface, Sanctus, and Hosanna in its preparation for the solemnity of the consecration. Its Canon likewise included the traditional elements of intercession, commemoration, and oblation, to which was added the invocation of the Holy Spirit, whilst the narrative of the Institution was presented in the very words of the New Testament. This was followed by the exhortation, confession, absolution, comfortable words, and prayer of humble access, preparatory to the communion of the people in both kinds during which communion the Agnus Dei was to be sung. The Mass concluded with a selected sentence from the New Testament, a prayer of thanksgiving, and a solemn benediction. The Holy Communion Office of 1552 differed considerably from its predecessor, omitting the Introit, Hosanna, Agnus Dei, the intercession for the departed, and the invocation of the Holy Spirit, whilst substituting for the ninefold Kyrie the Ten Commandments, and transposing the Gloria to the post-communion. Furthermore, the Canon was broken up into three separate prayers, that for the church militant here in earth (that is, the intercession for the living) following immediately after the offertory, the prayer of oblation following upon the communion of the people, and the prayer of consecration embracing the commemoration of the Redemption with the words of Institution. This change involved the further transposition of the exhortation, confession, absolution, comfortable words, and prayer of humble access before the consecration of the elements and in association now with the Sursum Corda and preface.

The second Prayer Book of Edward VI had little time to establish itself in general use owing to the death of the young king; but it formed the basis of the Elizabethan Act of Uniformity. In the 1549 Book the form of words said at the delivery of the elements to the communicants read: " The body of our Lord Jesus Christ which was given for thee—(The blood of our Lord Jesus Christ which was shed for thee)—preserve thy body and soul into everlasting life " ; whereas in the 1552 Book they read: " Take and eat this in remembrance that Christ died for thee and feed on him in thy heart by faith with thanksgiving: Drink this in remembrance that Christ's blood was shed for thee and be thankful." In the Elizabethan Prayer Book of 1559 these two forms were combined. Despite the considerable changes made in the second Edwardine Book and the omission of much enrichment retained in the first English Liturgy, its Communion Office was grounded upon Scripture, and upon primitive tradition as the reformers understood them.

Concurrently with the preparation of a vernacular Service Book went the provision in March 1550 of an English Ordinal. Its basis was the continuance of the three major Orders of Bishop, Priest, and Deacon, whilst abolishing the various minor orders. This gave unequivocal evidence of the continuity of the Church of England with historic Christian tradition in respect of the ministry. Moreover, admission to each grade of the ministry was by imposition of hands with prayer; the bishop alone laying his hands upon those to be made deacons, the bishop and attendant presbyters sharing the imposition of hands upon those to be ordered priests, and three bishops being requisite for the consecration of a bishop. In the ordination of priests and in the consecration of bishops, the *Veni Creator* was recited; whilst at the actual imposition of hands, in the case of priests, the words " receive the Holy Ghost " were pronounced, followed by the bestowal of power to forgive and retain sins (John xx. 22–3), and to administer the Word and Sacraments, and in the case of bishops the words " take the Holy Ghost " were followed by a reference to the duty of stirring up the grace of God given by imposition of hands (2 Tim. i. 6–7). The English Ordinal from the first omitted the use of unction, the vesting of the deacon with dalmatic and stole, of the priest with chasuble and stole, and of the bishop with ring and mitre. At the ordination of priests it omitted also the words " Receive the power to offer sacrifice to God and to celebrate Masses both for the living and the dead ". The revised Ordinal in the second Prayer Book also surceased the delivery by the bishop to the priest of " the chalice or cuppe with the breade ", and that by the archbishop to the bishop of the pastoral staff, which had been retained in the first English Ordinal; though the delivery of the Book was retained throughout, and instead of the Book of the Gospels, the deacon received the New Testament, and the priest and bishop the whole Bible.

In the exhortation by the bishop to those about to be ordered priest, they were enjoined to be studious " in reading and learning the Holy Scriptures " and in " daily reading and weighing of the Scriptures " ; whilst in the question addressed to them in their public examination before the imposition of hands, the bishop likewise enquired if they were " persuaded that the Holy Scriptures contain sufficiently all doctrine required of necessity for external salvation through faith in Jesus Christ ", if they were " determined out of the said Scriptures to instruct the people committed to their charge, and to teach nothing as required of necessity to eternal salvation, but that which they shall be persuaded may be concluded and proved by the Scripture ", and if they would " be diligent in prayers and in reading of the Holy Scriptures, and in such studies as help to the knowledge of the same " ? Similar enquiry was addressed by the archbishop to the bishop-elect before his consecration, whether the latter would " faithfully exercise himself in the same Holy Scriptures, and call upon God by prayer for the true understanding of the same ", so that he "may be able by them to teach and exhort with wholesome doctrine, and to withstand and convince the gain- . sayer ". At the delivery of the Bible the archbishop exhorted the bishop to " give heed unto reading, exhortation, and doctrine; think upon the things contained in this Book ". The Anglican Ordinal brought the ministry of the Word and Sacraments into close and indissoluble association, exhorting the priest to be " a faithful dispenser of the Word of God and of His holy Sacraments ", and giving to him authority " to preach the Word of God and to administer the Holy Sacraments " in the congregation to which he should go. The Ordinal was modelled, as its authors understood them, upon Scripture interpreted by primitive tradition.

The same characteristic governed doctrinal standards. The Elizabethan Act of Uniformity accepted as its definition of heresy that which " heretofore have been determined, ordered, or judged to be heresy by the authority of the canonical Scriptures, or by the first four General Councils, or any of them, or by another General Council wherein the same was declared heresy by the express and plain words of the said canonical Scriptures ". The same principles were reaffirmed in the Thirty-nine Articles of Religion; where in the VIIIth Article the Apostles', Nicene, and Athanasian Creeds were received, " for they may be proved by most certain warrants of Holy Scripture "; in the XXth Article the authority of the Church was interpreted in such wise that the Church cannot " ordain anything that is contrary to God's Word written ", but its office is that of " a witness and keeper of Holy Writ "; and in the XXIst Article the authority of General Councils was brought to the same test whether what is ordained by them as necessary to salvation " be taken out of Holy Scripture ".[1] The Articles of Religion defined also the position of the Church of England in regard to those matters of controversy which had agitated the

---

[1] Article XX. *Ecclesiae non licet quicquam instituere, quod verbo Dei adversetur neque unum Scripturae locum sic exponere potest, ut alteri contradicat. Quare licet Ecclesia sit divinorum librorum testis, et conservatrix, attamen ut adversus eos nihil decernere, neque robur habent, neque authoritatem, nisi ostendi possint a sacris literis esse desumpta.*

reformed churches of the continent. The XXVth Article
defined Sacraments in careful terms such as to exclude Zwingli's
conception by its affirmation that they " be not only badges or
tokens of Christian men's profession, but rather they be certain
and sure witnesses, and effectual signs of grace and God's good
will towards us, by the which He doth work invisibly in us, and
doth not only quicken, but also strengthen and confirm our
Faith in Him ". Similarly Article XXVIII declared the Lord's
Supper to be " a Sacrament of our Redemption by Christ's
death; insomuch that to such as rightly, worthily, and with faith
receive the same, the Bread which we break is a partaking of
the Body of Christ, and likewise the Cup of blessing is a partaking of the Blood of Christ ". The article rejected Transubstantiation, and affirmed that " the Body of Christ is given,
taken, and eaten in the Supper only after an heavenly and
spiritual manner; and the mean whereby the Body of Christ is
received and eaten in the Supper is Faith ".[1] In the section on
Sacraments added to the Catechism in 1604 the Eucharist was
said to have been ordained " for the continual remembrance of
the sacrifice of the death of Christ and of the benefits which we
receive thereby "; its outward part, or *signum*, defined as " bread
and wine ", its inward part or thing signified or *res*, as " the
Body and Blood of Christ which are verily and indeed taken
and received by the faithful in the Lord's Supper "; and " the
benefits whereof we are partakers thereby ", or *virtus*, as " the
strengthening and refreshing of our souls by the Body and
Blood of Christ as our bodies are by the Bread and Wine ".

---

[1] Article XXV. *Sacramenta a Christo instituta, non tantum sunt notae pro-
fessionis Christianorum, sed certa quaedam potius testimonia, et efficacia signa
gratiae, atque bonae in nos voluntatis Dei, per quae invisibiliter ipse in nos
operatur, nostramque fidem in se non solo excitat, verumetiam confirmat.*

Article XXVIII. *Coena Domini non est tantum signum mutuae benevolentiae
Christianorum inter sese, verum potius est Sacramentum nostrae per mortem
Christi redemptionis. Atque adeo, rite, digne, et cum fide sumentibus, panis
quem fragimus est communicatio corporis Christi; similiter poculum benedict-
ionis, et communicatio sanguinis Christi . . .*

*Corpus Christi datur, accipitur, et manducatur in Coena, tantum coelesti, et
spirituali ratione. Medium autem quo corpus Christi accipitur, et manducatur
in Coena, fides est.*

In Article XXXI [1] the corruptions and abuses associated with the multiplication of private Masses in which it was popularly believed that " the priest did offer Christ for the quick and dead, to have remission of pain or guilt " were repudiated.

In regard to the burning controversies concerning justification, Article XI declared that justification proceeded only from the merit of Christ by faith, and not from our own works or deserving, and it adopted the Lutheran phrase that we are justified *sola fide*; but in so doing used it to contradict the doctrine of salvation by works, as the following Article further developed by its insistence that, though good works are not the ground of justification yet, they are the *fructus fidei* and flow necessarily from a true faith. Similarly Article IX concerning Original Sin, and Article XVII on Predestination and Election adopted a mediatising position; the former merely affirming that man " is very far gone (*quam longissime distet*) from original righteousness ", but not totally corrupt; whilst the latter, after defining predestination to life, laid down the principle that " we must receive God's promises in such wise as they be generally set forth to us in Holy Scripture "; so that its standpoint concerning predestination and election was accepted equally in the eighteenth century by so ardent an Arminian as John Wesley and by so vehement a Calvinist as George Whitefield.

The ideal of the English Reformers, as of Calvin himself, in respect of public worship was the assembling of the church every Sunday for the service of Holy Communion. The Anglican Prayer Books embodied explicitly the standard of the unity of the homiletic and liturgical elements in the Eucharist, at which alone provision was made for the preaching of a sermon. The prescription of special collect, epistle, and gospel for each Sunday of the Christian year enforced further their intention; and thus the Word and Sacrament were united. But the conservatism of the laity in adhering to their medieval custom of infrequent communion frustrated the Reformers. The rubric in the First Edwardine Prayer Book that " the priest on the weke

[1] Article XXXI. . . . *unde missarum sacrificia, quibus, vulgo dicebatur, sacerdotem offere Christum, in remissionem poenae, aut culpae, pro vivis et defunctis. blasphema figmenta sunt, et perniciosae imposturae.*

daie shall forbeare to celebrate the Communion except he have some that will communicate with hym ", and the corresponding rubric in 1552 that " there shall be no Communion except four or three at least communicate with the priest " led to the disappearance not only of the daily, but also of the weekly Eucharist. Even the provision by rubric of the First English Prayer Book for the presence of some communicants each Sunday by requiring that " some one at the least of that house in every parish to whom by course . . . it apperteyneth to offer for the charges of the Communion, or some other whom they shall provide to offer for them, shall receive the holy Communion with the prieste ", failed in its purpose. Thus the weekly Eucharist intended by the Prayer Book to be celebrated with sermon and communicants every Sunday gave place to the classical Ante-Communion of the Anglican tradition, comparable with the *missa catechumenorum* of the early Church or the *missa sicca* of the medieval Church. The only advance made on medieval custom was the requirement of the laity by the Second Prayer Book to communicate ' at the least three times in the year '. Thus at most a monthly Communion was secured in populous parishes, whilst the general standard sank to the quarterly Sacrament. In the seventeenth century one of the points of difference between high- and low-churchmen was that the former, after reading Matins at their prayer desk, proceeded to the Holy Table for the Ante-Communion, whilst the latter read the whole service from the desk. The frustration of the ideal of the Reformers in divine service of the fusion of the didactic or hortatory with the liturgical elements in worship was the most serious failure of the Reformation, in England as elsewhere.

In like manner the First English Prayer Book required the celebrant to " put upon him the vesture appointed for that ministration, that is to say, a white Albe plain with a vestment or Cope" and the assistant-clergy to wear " albes with tunacles". The Second Book reversed this injunction by ordering that the Minister " at the time of the Communion . . . shall use neither Alb, Vestment, nor Cope, but being archbishop or bishop, he shall have and wear a rochet, and being a priest or deacon, he shall have and wear a surplice only ". In 1559 the Elizabethan Prayer Book added a new rubric to the effect that " the Minister at the time of the Communion . . . shall use such ornaments in the Church as were in use by authority of Parliament in the second year of King Edward VI, according to the Act of Parliament at the beginning of this Book ". The Act thus referred to, the Elizabethan Act of Uniformity of 1559, decreed that " such ornaments of the Church and of the ministers thereof, shall be retained and be in use, as was in the Church of England by authority of Parliament in the second year of the reign of King Edward VI, until other order shall be therein taken by the authority of the Queen's majesty ". Much controversy has centred round the interpretation of the Elizabethan rubric and Act of Parliament. But although the general intention of the Queen and her advisers seems to have been towards the retention of the traditional Eucharistic vestments, this standard proved so impossible of enforcement that the *Advertisements* of Archbishop Parker in 1566 endeavoured only to insist upon the wearing of the surplice, and even this requirement was hotly opposed and resisted. The consequence of which was that in external ceremonies the Anglican parish churches of sixteenth- and seventeenth-century England approximated more nearly to the reformed churches of the Continent in their bareness and simplicity than to those of the Lutheran confession. The surplice became the customary vesture for the Holy Communion, and with the prescription in the 82nd Canon of the Canons of 1604 " that the Ten Commandments be set upon the east end of every church and chapel, where the people may best see and read the same, and other chosen sentences written upon the walls of the said churches and chapels " (which additions usually embraced the Lord's Prayer, and the Apostles' Creed as well as Scriptural sentences), Anglican worship both amongst high- and low-churchmen became characterised by an austere severity.

The Elizabethan Church had of necessity to avail itself at first in its episcopate of the services of the returned Continental exiles, many of whom were luke-warm in admiration of the principles of its Liturgy, and nearly all paid great deference, as their correspondence indicates, to the judgment and criticism of

Calvin. At first, therefore, the Elizabethan settlement was on the defensive, but with the gradual establishment of its position a more confident spirit animated its bishops and clergy, and the task of expounding its position as standing in the true *via media* between the extremes of Rome and Geneva, and appealing to the Bible, the Fathers, and the œcumenical Councils, was undertaken. The classical apology was that of Hooker, at the end of the sixteenth century, which championed its character as reformed and catholic, and laid its bases broadly upon the testimony of Scripture, tradition, and reason. With the development of these tendencies the Church had to face the sharpened and determined assault of the Presbyterian party within its communion. At first the contest centred on the vesture of the clergy, within church and outdoors, but it changed soon to the serious ground of a demand by Thomas Cartwright for the remodelling of the Church of England according to the Genevan standard of a Presbyterian ministry and the directory of public worship. With the resolve of the Queen and the episcopate to suppress this movement, there appeared the dual phenomena of attempts to introduce the Presbyterian discipline inside the established church and of the rise of dissenting congregations which actually forsook its outward communion. Thus the first Presbyterian congregation was set up at Wandsworth in 1572. In general, however, Presbyterians and Anglicans were drawn together by their common belief in a national church, and the number of formal secessions from the Church of England on the part of Presbyterians was small.

More threatening to this conviction of both was the emergence of the movement of Independency, with its insistence upon the conception of " the church planted or gathered " as being " a company or number of Christians or believers, which, by a willing covenant made with their God, are under the government of God and Christ, and keep His laws in one holy communion ". In practice Independency asserted the autonomy and complete self-government of each several congregation and denied the competence of the civil power to exercise authority in religion. This movement, led first by Robert Browne and afterwards by John Penry, Henry Barrow, and John Greenwood, it being noteworthy that Cambridge nurtured most of the Separatist leaders, presented an equal challenge to Anglican and Presbyterian, and could make no terms with any national church. From the same stem of Independency there sprang the Baptist congregations, which incurred much unmerited suspicion in England at first because of the traditional aversion to Anabaptism, but continued to assert their position, although divided internally into an Arminian and a Calvinist section. Thus the Anglican ideal of a single reformed church, representing the nation in its religious aspect and comprising an identity of citizens and churchmen, failed altogether of realisation. With the advance of the seventeenth century, and particularly during the Commonwealth, the influence and numbers of the Independents greatly increased, and this period was marked by the emergence of another sect, that of the Quakers, which evoked at first an almost universal antipathy by reason of its repudiation alike of an official ministry and of all sacraments.

Throughout the seventeenth century the hope of a comprehension of Presbyterian and Anglican within the fold of a single established and national church persisted, surviving even the setbacks of the Hampton Court and Savoy conferences, but failing finally to achieve its objective in 1689. Thenceforth the Church of England maintained its position as the established church, but religious toleration, though unattended by civil equality, was granted to orthodox Trinitarian Protestant dissenters and Quakers. Thus the Reformation movements in England resulted in the same divisions within the State as in France, the Empire, and Switzerland. Despite the failure of the Tudor ideal of a national church coterminous with the civil kingdom, the English Reformation had its peculiar and abiding witness in the *Ecclesia Anglicana*, distinct alike from the Roman Church of the Counter-Reformation era and from the several Protestant churches of Europe, Lutheran, Zwinglian, and reformed, and developing a positive and definite character and position between the Papalist and Puritan interpretations of Christianity.

CHAPTER V

The Counter-Reformation

THE necessity for reform of the Church in head and members had been a commonplace amongst churchmen of all degrees during the century preceding the Reformation movements. Nor may it be forgotten that the leaders of the reforming movements which issued in separation from Rome had been themselves bred within its communion, and were largely clergy, either of the regular or secular orders. Moreover, some of the mystical and spiritual tendencies, such as the *Devotio Moderna*, the German mystics, and the revival of Augustinianism, which had led rebellious and ardent spirits to schism, were capable also of generating a revived spiritual zeal within the Roman Church upon which reform might be based. Evidences of the operation of such influences were seen in the attempts towards reform of the existing religious orders, of which the Capuchin movement was the most noteworthy, in the experiments towards creating congregations of secular clergy, typified by the Barnabite, Somaschi, and Theatine congregations in Italy, and most famous of all, in the foundation of the Oratory of Divine Love towards the end of the pontificate of Leo X. The object of all these foundations was the encouragement and restoration amongst the clergy, secular and religious, of spiritual zeal and holiness, and especially the regeneration of the parochial clergy, so that many of the abuses both of life and doctrine which had been the butt of satirists might be removed. Together with religious renovation there went some degree of theological innovation, seen in the revived study of Augustine which naturally threw into prominence the doctrine of Justification. Amongst the leaders of these several movements were names so eminent in the history of the Roman Church as Reginald Pole, afterwards Archbishop of Canterbury and Cardinal, Giovanni Matteo Giberti, afterwards Bishop of Verona, Giovanni Pietro Caraffa, afterwards Pope Paul IV, Gasparo Contarini, a Venetian noble-man, afterwards Cardinal, and Giovanni Morone, afterwards Bishop of Modena and Cardinal.

In Italy itself, therefore, there were germinating the seeds of a potential religious revival. The peculiar problems of Italy, how-ever, were associated with the Papacy and its Curia, which, whilst offering a welcome to these tendencies towards spiritual regeneration amongst the clergy, were naturally averse from schemes of radical reform which would threaten the various vested interests concentrated in the papal administration. " The moral transformation of Rome," it has been observed, " was a slow process, perceptible only over a long period." The grave responsibility of the Papacy was its delay in taking measures to meet the growing menace of the revolt from Rome until so large a part of Christian Europe had seceded irrevocably from its allegiance. The extent of necessary reform found expression indeed in emphatic terms in the report presented in 1537 by a commission of nine appointed by Paul III, under the title *Con-silium delectorum cardinalium et aliorum praelatorum de emendenda ecclesia.* The document was as unsparing in its catalogue of abuses and ascription of responsibility as the most ardent reformer could desire, for it laid the blame at the door of the Papacy itself and particularly reprobated the practice of issuing dispensations from the canon law in return for fees. It continued to specify the necessity for clerical residence, for the reform of religious houses, for the better education of the clergy, for the restoration of episcopal authority, and for the reform of abuses connected with indulgences. The indictment, so far as concerned abuses of administration, was severe; but although a series of com-missions to consider reforms based on the report was appointed, nothing was done to accelerate their deliberations. The Papacy was not sufficiently alert to redeem the times whilst the Protestant rebellions were still within negotiating distance, and the result was that when reformation was taken in hand, the possibility of reconciliation was slight, if still existent.

The fact that the sessions of the Council of Trent did not begin before 1545 was itself sufficient measure of the supineness and antipathy of Rome to any thoroughgoing reform. The

Apostolic See, however, had some reason for its hesitancy to commit the remedying of things amiss to the agency of a general council. In the first place the appeal of almost all the Reformers was from the present corrupt Pope and Curia to a future general council, representative of all Christendom, amongst which they certainly reckoned themselves. Further, the last experiment in conciliar government had come sufficiently near to threatening the entire fabric of papal supremacy as to make Rome more than suspicious of ever allowing a council to assemble again. The memories of Constance and Basle did not encourage a repetition of the venture. Even if an ecclesiastical majority at the council could be secured to the papal cause by a preponderance of Italian bishops in sufficient numbers to carry the vote in divisions, the attitude of the civil rulers might be more difficult to circumvent. The rights of the Emperor in general councils had a respectable historical basis in antiquity, whilst the Emperor Sigismund had played an important part in the fifteenth-century councils. The Emperor Charles V at the present juncture, though a zealous advocate of a council, desired it to be free from papal control, meeting outside Italy, and seeking fairly for some basis of compromise with Protestant representatives. The attitude of the kings of France varied with the exigencies of their internal policy. But both emperor and French king could be relied upon to bring to the forefront at any council the question of reform of the Papacy and Curia, so that the policy of the Holy See and that of the civil rulers would be difficult to harmonise in this respect. Moreover, the dynastic rivalry of Habsburg and Valois made impossible the assembling of an ecclesiastical council until peace had been made between them, a cause of delay for which Rome was not responsible.

Amid such circumstances it was perhaps less remarkable that the sessions of the Council of Trent were so protracted and interrupted, than that the council succeeded in meeting at all and in transacting so great a volume of business despite the many factors inimical to its progress. Its first two periods, embracing the years 1545-8 and 1551-2, were snatched from the temporary truce in politics between 1544 and 1552; whilst the resumption of its meetings in 1562 was made possible by the settlement of

Cateau-Cambrésis in 1559. Notwithstanding, the fact that the sessions of the council did not begin until 1545 was itself of great significance in its history. By that date the hope of reconciling the Protestant churches to the See of Rome was slight, and the opportunity of speedy action before schism had become irreparable had been allowed to pass unused. By that time also the movement within the Roman Church for a compromise with the Protestants by means of such disciplinary relaxations as the allowance of the Mass in the vernacular, the giving of the chalice to the laity, and the marriage of clergy, and of doctrinal adjustments upon the points of justification, and the Sacraments, had been fatally weakened by the deaths of Contarini in 1542 and of Giberti in 1543 and by the gradual defection of Caraffa. On the other hand, two of the agencies through which the results of the council were to be carried into effect had already been created, the Society of Jesus in 1540, and the Inquisition in 1542, of which the influence of members of the former, the Jesuit theologians, Laynez and Salmeron, at the council was considerable.

Despite the difficulties surrounding its inception and continuance, the Council of Trent was the most influential of the several forces which moulded the Counter-Reformation movement within the Roman Church. From its decrees there emerged a definition of doctrine which effectively excluded the possibility of reconciliation with the Protestants, and a series of administrative reforms which removed the worst abuses of the Church. It has to be remarked, however, that the course of its proceedings demonstrated that the Church of Rome, no less than the Protestant churches, had to pay continuous regard to the policy of civil princes and to adjust its own programme in accordance with their wishes, and that the prelates and theologians of the Roman Catholic faith were no less subject to the human infirmities of quarrelsomeness and temper than the protagonists of the Reformed Confessions. The relations of the Papacy and the Emperor Charles V throughout the first two periods of conciliar sessions were always delicate, so that an attempt by the Papacy to translate the council from Trent to Bologna had to be abandoned in face of imperial threats. Similarly when the renewal of its sessions was adumbrated by Pius IV, much difficulty was encountered in circumventing the opposition of the emperor Ferdinand I and the king of France to regarding the new sessions as a continuation of the former meetings, since their desires were for a new council and a renewed attempt towards conciliation with the Protestants. Towards the end of the Council, however, the tables were turned; and the Papacy had recourse to its traditional policy of seeking private arrangements with the emperor and the French king in order to bring the conciliar sessions to an end, and to prevent the possibility of an assertion of the inherent authority and jurisdiction of the episcopate *divino jure*, by virtue of direct Dominical appointment, against the claims of the Papacy to mediate this authority and jurisdiction from Christ to the bishops. Once again the diplomacy of Rome to rid itself of a general council was invoked with success, as had been the case at Basle in the fifteenth century. Within the conciliar meetings themselves the Papacy relied upon the predominant numbers of Italian bishops, subject to its influence and sometimes to financial pressure. At the outset the Council resolved not to repeat the experiment tried at Constance of voting by nations, and also to restrict the vote to bishops and heads of religious orders whilst rejecting the claim of absent bishops to vote by proxy. During the sessions of the last period of the council, after its revocation in 1562, in point of fact a large majority of prelates attending were Italian, with minority groups of Spanish and French bishops, but very few of other nationalities. These considerations do not detract from the importance of the theological decrees of the council, though they furnish abundant evidence of the influence of the political diplomacy of the Papacy, which secured its special triumph, as has been observed, in " the very delicate negotiations before, during, and after the council ".

From the moment of its assembly at Trent in 1545 the Council had to determine an order of priority between reform of abuses and definition of dogma. Pope Paul III was resolved that doctrine should take precedence, whilst the Emperor Charles V and the Spanish episcopate were equally determined on reform. A compromise was secured by which dogma and reform should be treated at the same time by the separate commissions of the

Council, and should come before the full Council in alternation. The organisation of procedure followed the general rules of three divisions of the Council, to which were submitted the drafts of each question to be discussed, which had been prepared by theologians and canonists, a general congregation of the whole synod to receive and discuss the reports of each of its three sections, and a solemn session of the Council for the promulgation of decrees. Although the Council had resolved to treat doctrine and reform in alternation, it will be convenient for purposes of clarity and continuity to consider first its dogmatic definitions and then the question of reform.

At the outset the Council considered the Rule of Faith in the Church, reaffirming the Nicene Creed, in significant phrase, as symbolum fidei quo sancta *Romana* ecclesia utitur. It then passed to consider the sources of religious belief and doctrine, defining these as the Scriptures and unwritten Traditions, taught by Christ Himself or by the Holy Spirit, and declaring that the Church received both sources as of equal authority and with equal reverence (*pari pietatis affectu ac reverentia suscepit et veneratur*). The decree continued further to pronounce the Vulgate as the authoritative version (*haec ipsa vetus et vulgata editio . . . pro authentica habeatur*), and the Church as the sole interpreter of the Bible. The importance of these initial decrees can hardly be exaggerated. The equation of Scripture and Tradition went far in itself to make reconciliation with the reformed churches impossible. Not only did it present the direct negative to the principle that " the Bible, and the Bible only, is the religion of Protestants " (though the difficulties of this position were evident amongst the Protestants themselves), but by placing the two sources on a parity it ruled out the position adopted later in the XXth Article of the Anglican Articles of Religion, in which the Church was affirmed to be a witness and keeper (*testis et conservatrix*) of the Scriptures, though lacking authority to prescribe anything to be believed of necessity for salvation which could not be proved therefrom. Moreover, this definition concerning the equal authority of Scripture and Tradition was of evident importance in approaching such questions as the number and Dominical institution of the Sacraments. In regard to the declaration that the Vulgate was the authoritative version of the Bible, even in 1546 this decree was contradictory to the best scholarship of the day, and represented a triumph of conservatism over learning.

The Council passed next to the question of Original Sin, and thence to the related problem of Justification. The decree on Original Sin affirmed a change in human nature for the worse (*in deterius commutatum*) as a consequence of the Fall, and that a taint was left even in the baptised, which *concupiscentia* was not sin, but the consequence of sin and an inclination thereto (*ex peccato est et ad peccatum inclinat*). The debates preceding the issue of the decree on Justification were long and intense, for the importance of the subject in relation to the Protestants was evident, and on the other hand there were few definitions to guide the steps of the fathers. Much time was given to discussion of the difference between inherent and imputed Justification; and the weight of the Jesuit theologians was cast against the latter. The final decree was a lengthy and careful document, embracing sixteen chapters followed by thirty-three canons. The historian of the Papacy, Pastor, pronounced it " a masterpiece of theology, formulating with clearness and precision the standard of Catholic truth as distinguished from Pelagian error on the one hand and Protestant on the other ". His summary of its contents may be quoted.

> Starting from the axiom that neither the heathen by their natural powers, nor the Jews by the Mosaic law are capable of participation, i.e., of reaching a state of grace and of adoption as children of God, the decree first of all insists that Christ alone is the salvation of the world through the communication of the merits of His sufferings, and that only for those who believe in Him, and have been born again in Him by baptism. In adults justification has its beginning in the calling of God through prevenient grace without any supernatural merit on the part of man. The latter can resist grace or co-operate with it. In both cases there is the exercise of free will, but the co-operation is also conditioned by grace.
>
> With justification man receives not merely the forgiveness of sins but is also inwardly sanctified. This renewal also is not merely imputed as something adhering to man from without but is a deep inward process fundamentally transforming the soul. Faith, however, is not alone

sufficient for justification; it must be accompanied by hope and love, and, as the Scripture says, faith certainly must work by love, since faith without works is dead. Faith working by love in a constant state of grace through the following of the commandments of God and the Church results in a continual advance from virtue to virtue.

In opposition to the Protestant assertion of an absolute assurance of salvation it was laid down as Catholic doctrine that no one in this life can fathom the secret of his predestination by God, and, apart from a special revelation, know of a certainty that he is of the number of the elect.

The decree thus rejected the teaching of Luther and Calvin upon justification by faith alone and election. It can hardly be denied that in its careful balance and proportion of the different elements in the doctrine of grace, it constituted a sounder theological definition than that of the German and Swiss Reformers. Modern Protestant scholars, indeed, have been ready to admit " the service rendered to truth and common sense by the Council of Trent when it repudiated the more emphatic expressions of that quasi-Pauline determinism to which the great Reformers were so addicted ". Notwithstanding, the decree took a further step towards making impossible a compromise and reconciliation with the Protestants, such as had seemed possible by the agreement on Justification reached by the conference at Ratisbon in 1541.

From the determination of this issue the Council passed to define the doctrine of the Sacraments. Its decree *De Sacramentis* affirmed that the sacraments were seven in number, neither more nor less, and were all instituted by Christ, a position unacceptable to all the reformed churches. It declared that they contained the grace which they signified, and that they conferred this grace *ex opere operato*, that is, not *ex opere operantis* but in virtue of Christ's promise and institution. Three of these sacraments, baptism, confirmation and order, conferred an indelible character and could not be repeated. From these general statements the Council proceeded to define more exactly its doctrine of each sacrament. The decree on the Eucharist comprised eight chapters followed by eleven canons. It declared that after the consecration of the elements " our Lord Jesus Christ, very God and very man, is verily, really, and substantially contained under the species of bread and wine ". (*Dominum nostrum Jesum Christum verum Deum atque hominem vere, realiter ac substantialiter sub specie illarum rerum sensibilium contineri.*) Accordingly the nature of this change in the sacramental elements was properly called Transubstantiation; and the highest form of worship, such as is due to God, should be paid to the Sacrament by the faithful (*latriae cultum, qui vero Deo debetur, huic sanctissimo sacramento in veneratione exhibeant*). The eleven canons following the definition formally anathematised the tenets of Luther, Zwingli, Calvin and the Anabaptists, denouncing all attempts to deny worship to the sacramental elements when reserved or carried in procession, and all opinions which restricted the real presence to the purpose of actual communion and denied it to the reserved Sacrament. Between the issue of this decree on the Eucharist and the completion of the work of definition by that on the Sacrifice of the Mass, there intervened the long prorogation of the conciliar sessions produced by the international situation. Whereas the former decree was declared on 11th October, 1551, the latter was not accepted until 27th September, 1562.

The *Doctrina de sacrificio Missae* was of equal, if not greater, importance with the decree on the Eucharist, for most of the criticisms of the Reformers had sprung from the corruptions and abuses associated with the doctrine of the Eucharistic sacrifice. The decree consisted of nine chapters, followed by nine canons. The first chapter affirmed that Christ at the Last Supper gave power and command to His apostles (whom He *then* made priests) and their successors in the priesthood, to offer His body and blood under the species of bread and wine, thus leaving to His Church a visible sacrifice (*visibile sacrificium*), by means of which the power (*virtus*) of the sacrifice completed on the Cross (which was represented in the Mass) was applied to the remission of those sins committed daily by men. Since in the sacrifice of the Mass the self-same Christ is contained and is bloodlessly offered, as on the altar of the Cross, the sacrifice is truly propitiatory (*vere propitiatorium*); and, according to the tradition of the apostles, it is fitly offered for the sins, punishments, satisfactions, and other needs of the living and also of the dead in

Christ not yet fully purged.[1] Moreover, although it is to be wished that the faithful should be present and communicate sacramentally at every Mass, yet those Masses at which the priest alone communicates sacramentally are not to be condemned as private and illicit (*privatas et illicitas*), but approved and commended as truly public, forasmuch as the people communicate spiritually and the public minister celebrates them not for himself but for all the faithful. The Mass also should not be said in the vulgar tongue. In the appended canons a specified series of contrary opinions were anathematised; particularly the denial that in the Mass there was offered to God a true and proper sacrifice (*verum et proprium sacrificium*), and the opinion that the sacrifice of the Mass was only a sacrifice of praise and thanksgiving, or a mere commemoration of the sacrifice offered on the Cross, and not a propitiatory sacrifice, or that it benefited only those present and ought not to be offered for the sins, punishment, satisfactions, and other needs of the living and the dead.[2]

The theological language of the decree was carefully chosen, for the propitiatory character of the sacrifice of the Mass may be a borrowed propitiation from that of the Cross. But it is difficult to interpret its intention otherwise than as not only approving the continuation of private Masses, but allowing the perpetuation of those erroneous ideas of their nature popularly associated with private Masses offered for the quick and the dead, which ideas the conciliar definition " covertly shielded as with the fringe of its mantle ". Evidently the decree was designed, not to commend itself to the Reformers nor to prepare the ground for an agreement, but to confirm the traditional practice of the Roman Church against contemporary criticism. Even the request for Mass in a language understanded of the people was refused.

Towards the end of the conciliar sessions decrees were passed

---

[1] *Quare non solum pro fidelium vivorum peccatis, poenis, satisfactionibus et aliis necessitatibus, sed et pro defunctis in Christo nondum ad plenum purgatis rite iuxta Apostolorum traditionem offertur.*

[2] *Si quis dixerit, missae sacrificium tantum esse laudis et gratiarum actionis, aut nudam commemorationem sacrificii in cruce peracti, non autem propitiatorium; vel soli prodesse sumenti; neque pro vivis et defunctis pro peccatis, poenis, satisfactionibus, et aliis necessitatibus, offeri debere, anathema sit.* (Canon 3.)

on other points of acute controversy, such as Purgatory, Indulgences, Relics and Images, and the Invocation of Saints. The decree on Purgatory affirmed that "there is a Purgatory, and the souls detained there are aided by the prayers of the faithful, and particularly by the acceptable sacrifice of the altar ".[1] It discouraged the discussion in popular gatherings of difficult questions concerning Purgatory which did not tend to edification, repudiated all mercenary associations of the doctrine, and ordered the episcopate to maintain the customary prayers of the faithful for the departed, by testament and otherwise, *missarum scilicet sacrificia* and other works of piety. The practice of the Invocation of Saints was based on the doctrine that "the Saints which reign with Christ offer to God their prayers for mankind, and that it is good and useful prayerfully to invoke them ".[2] Images were to be retained with the customary honour done to them, since such honour was offered to that which they represented. Indulgences were to be retained, but "all evil gains for the obtaining thereof" were condemned. The abolition of the office of Quaestor, or Indulgence-seller, name and thing, had been one of the few reforms actually carried into effect during the earlier sessions of the Council before its long suspension.

Reformation indeed had tarried long. The Emperor Ferdinand I, Francis II of France, and Philip II of Spain with the Spanish episcopate were zealous for ecclesiastical reform, but the Papacy was not so zealous; and, if reform were to be carried out, the Apostolic See preferred not to entrust it to the unregulated efforts of a council but to effect the desired end by private agreements with the several temporal rulers. Moreover, every attempt of the Council to grapple with the difficult problems of reform brought up the delicate question of the relation of the episcopate to the Papacy. In particular, when the importance of the residence of bishops within their diocese was debated, the allied question whether such residence was *divino jure* was also raised. The papal legates resisted attempts to deprive the Papacy of its

---

[1] *Purgatorium esse, animasque ibi detentas fidelium suffragiis, potentissimum vero acceptabili altaris sacrificio iuvari.*

[2] *Sanctos una cum Christo regnantes orationes suas pro hominibus Deo offere, bonum atque utile esse suppliciter eos iuvocare.*

powers of dispensation; and the affirmation of the Dominical appointment of the episcopate directly, and not indirectly, through the Papacy, though congenial to the non-Italian bishops present at the sessions, was never acceptable to Rome. Amid such obstacles the cause of reform advanced slowly.

Notwithstanding, considerable reforms were finally secured. " The abuses with which the Church had so often been reproached, are neither denied nor extenuated in the reform decrees. The very first sentence of the first decree candidly acknowledges that ecclesiastical discipline had become greatly relaxed, and that the morality of both clergy and people was at a low ebb." One expedient to meet the charges of immorality, that of the permission to the clergy to marry, was rejected, despite the advocacy of civil princes. The Council insisted upon the residence of each bishop in his diocese, and therefore forbade plurality of sees. The bishop, moreover, should have full and free authority in the administration of his diocese, and must be diligent in preaching, visitation, punishment of the guilty, and efforts to secure a worthy clergy. " The powers of bishops were strengthened against competing or exempt authorities—regulars, cathedral chapters, collegiate churches—in all directions except as against Rome." Each bishop should summon his clergy to a joint conference every year in a diocesan synod, and each metropolitan should hold a provincial synod every·three years. In order to raise the standard of piety and education amongst the secular parish priests, the powers of the bishop for their correction were reinforced; but, in the judgment of Pastor, " even more important than all these regulations for the prevention of unworthy persons being admitted into the ranks of the clergy, was the decree that in every diocese where there was no university a seminary should be established, where suitable young men were to be trained for the service of the sanctuary from their youth ". The subsequent history of these diocesan seminaries has emphasised the justice of this verdict. At the same time steps were taken to correct admitted abuses in the bestowal of benefices, such as expectations, the preferment of minors, and the conferment of canonries on such as would not be ordained or fulfil the duties of their office. " The true and intrinsic success of the

Council," concluded Pastor, " lay within the Church itself, though even there its decrees were not all of them carried into effect everywhere or at once. The law, for example, concerning provincial synods to be held every three years was nowhere observed, except perhaps by St. Charles Borromeo. In Germany the existing conditions made it necessary to unite several bishoprics in the hands of the son of some powerful prince. The reform of cathedral chapters remained a pious wish in many places, while even the important decree concerning the clerical seminaries was not at once carried out everywhere. A great number of abuses, however, were removed, many reforms were carried out at once in many districts, and in others more slowly."

The cumulative effects of the doctrinal and reforming decrees of Trent justify fully Pastor's verdict that " in spite of all disturbances, both from within and from without, in spite of all delays and obstructions, as well as the many human weaknesses which had come to light during the course of its proceedings, the Council had accomplished a mighty work and one of decisive importance ". It constituted in truth " at once a boundary and a landmark, at which opposing spirits must separate ", and it would be difficult to overstate its influence on the later history of the Roman Church. Its uncompromising rejection of all demands for restatement of doctrine had closed the door to the hope of reconciliation with the Protestant churches, from its first decree declaring the equal authority of Tradition and Scripture and affirming the authoritative character of the Vulgate. A comparison of the expectations entertained by the liberal churchmen of the Oratory of Divine Love and by the Emperor Charles V in respect of a general Council with the actual achievements of Trent demonstrated conclusively the unyielding spirit of the Tridentine decrees. Furthermore, the centralisation of the Papacy had been increased. The reform of the Curia had been undertaken by Pius IV, and not by the Council, and though the influence of the non-Italian bishops had prevented the recognition of the Pope as *rector universalis ecclesiae* and though no formal definition of the primacy of the Roman See was pronounced, in practice the Papacy had strengthened its control over the Church as a result of the Counter-Reformation.

Correspondent with the uncompromising rigidity of the Tridentine decrees were the instruments through which the Apostolic See proceeded to push home its aggressive campaign against the divided forces of Protestantism. Foremost amongst the agents of the revival of the Roman Church was indisputably the Society of Jesus, " the most powerful missionary organisation the world has ever seen ". Founded by Don Inigo Lopez de Recalde, of Loyola in Guipuscoa, a Spanish soldier severely wounded at Pampeluna in 1521 and thenceforward resolved to become a soldier of Christ, the Order received its constitution by a Bull of Paul III in 1540. From the first the Society was bound to the Papacy by a special vow of obedience, the importance of education was emphasised in its Rule, and the degree of authority exercised over members by the General of the Society was unprecedented in extent. The spiritual principles of the Order were drawn up by Ignatius himself in his *Spiritual Exercises*, a work of the utmost importance in devotional literature. The expansion of the Society was phenomenally rapid and widespread, whilst the uniformity of its methods created a homogeneity of religious practice and outlook which itself constituted a new means of unifying the Roman Church. Furthermore, the spirit of its founder and his Rule expressed an autocratic conception of the duty of absolute obedience to authority, whether of the General or the Pope, which was congenial to the *milieu* of the Counter-Reformation. The Jesuits exercised a profound influence in every sphere of social life. Their influence within the Council of Trent was great; and outside its sessions, one of their number, the German Canisius, rendered a service of almost equal importance in detaching the Emperor Ferdinand I from the support of the Council to the side of Pius IV The same Jesuit as Rector of the University of Ingolstadt converted an outpost of Protestantism into a stronghold of Roman Catholicism, whilst his catechism, the *Summa Doctrinae Christianae*, penetrated widely throughout Germany. As missionary agents beyond the confines of Europe, the Jesuits earned a reputation equalled only by their zeal and devotion.

Their influence was brought to bear upon the laity of Europe by missions and retreats. But of greater and more far-reaching importance than any of these varied activities was their service to the Roman Church in the field of education. The constitution of the Order had recognised the importance of the education of the young; and in addition to the efforts which they devoted to this work, they realised to the full the opportunities afforded by the establishment of diocesan seminaries for the training of the clergy. The influence and zeal of the Jesuits were ubiquitous throughout the Roman Church; and wherever they penetrated, they exalted the ideal of absolute and unquestioning obedience to the will of the Papacy.

Characteristic likewise of the spirit of the Roman Church of the Counter-Reformation were the instruments of the Inquisition and the Index, both fashioned anew before the conclusion of the Council. During the century preceding the Reformation, the medieval inquisition had appeared to be obsolete and antiquated. In 1477, however, the Papacy at the request of Spain had authorised its introduction into that kingdom, where it became a formidable instrument of royal persecution. Its success in Spain suggested to Paul III, strongly supported by Ignatius Loyola, the idea of reconstituting and renewing the Inquisition in Rome to supervise the entire Roman Church. Accordingly the Bull *Licet initio* of 1542 established the Holy Office of the Universal Church. Though its powers and authority were œcumenical in theory, in practice its work was confined chiefly to the Italian peninsula itself, where it was an effective weapon in the suppression of heresy; for in the Spanish peninsula the royal inquisition needed no reinforcement from Rome, whilst the kings of France refused to allow its introduction in their kingdom.

Similarly the Index, though a reply to the new challenge presented to the Roman Church by the widespread dissemination of religious books and tracts made possible by the invention of printing, was of doubtful efficacy in practice though not in intention. During the first half of the sixteenth century papal encouragement had led to the compilation at Louvain, Cologne, Toledo, and Paris of various local lists of books dangerous to

the beliefs and morals of the faithful; but the first Papal Index
was published by Paul IV in 1559. This *Index Librorum Pro-
hibitorum* evoked much criticism and opposition; and the Council
of Trent was so conscious of its imperfections as to appoint a
commission to revise it. The report of this commission was
published by the Papacy in 1564, and the " Tridentine " Index
secured a considerable acceptance in countries faithful to the
Roman obedience, notably in Portugal, Belgium, Bavaria, and
parts of Italy. Its contents were subject to several subsequent
revisions, and the Index issued by Clement VIII in 1596 remained
the standard for a century and a half. At its best the Index could
achieve only a negative success; and the best antidote to heretical
books was constructive teaching and writing on the part of champions of the Roman Church.

In this field also the result of the Counter-Reformation was a
notable revival of religion and theology. Rome itself became
again a centre of learning and scholarship; and in the historical
sphere the *Annals* of Baronius the Oratorian were worthy to
stand beside the Lutheran *Centuries of Magdeburg*. New editions
of the Fathers and of the Septuagint were published; and attempts
to improve the text of the Vulgate received papal encouragement. Sanctity of life was again recognised as a characteristic
feature of the Roman Church, and was exhibited by individuals
of such differing gifts as Charles Borromeo, Francis de Sales, and
Philip Neri. Amongst controversialists, engaged in the dust and
heat of debate with the reformed churches, Bellarmine obtained
an admitted pre-eminence. Nor may the emergence of a rich
school of French mystical writers in the seventeenth century be
forgotten in recounting the history of the Counter-Reformation
triumphs. No longer was the *sancta Romana ecclesia* a byword
of abuses and corruption. Its missionaries were conquering
heathen lands and reconquering parts of lapsed Europe. Above
all, in the Society of Jesus the Papacy had found an agent of
defence, education, missionary activity, and influence unequalled
since Gregory the Great's recognition of the potentialities of the
monks of St. Benedict.

A heavy price had been paid, however, for the Counter-
Reformation, and especially in the spirit of rigidity which

informed the decrees of the Council of Trent and the Jesuit Order. Roman Catholic historians have admitted the narrowness of temper and rigidity of dogma which resulted from the sixteenth-century controversies. "Centralisation, uniformity, rigour marked the features of Catholicism in convalescence"; and this atmosphere "naturally conditioned the attitude of Counter-Reformation Catholicism to science, learning, and culture in general". Not only was much of the intellectual spaciousness and freedom of the thirteenth century, the golden age of medieval Catholicism, lost; but Trent stamped upon the doctrinal system of the Roman Church a rigidity which proved increasingly hampering. The Jesuit emphasis upon the duty of absolute obedience led to results in the intellectual sphere almost more disastrous than in the moral. The hope of an œcumenical council which would effect a reconciliation between the reformed and Roman churches and recover the unity of Christendom under the ægis of a liberal Catholicism was indefinitely postponed by the decrees of Trent. The Church of Rome gained much in interior reform, in tightening of discipline, and definition of orthodoxy from the Counter-Reformation; but it emerged bearing the continuing aspect of a besieged and beleaguered city.

CHAPTER VI

THE CRISIS AND THE RESPONSE: GAIN AND LOSS

AT the accession of Pius IV to the papal throne in 1559, the
future of Europe in religion seemed to belong to the Protestant churches, which appeared not yet to have attained the
limit of their advance, much less to be in prospect of losing some
of the ground already won to the forces of a reformed and aggressive Church of Rome. Yet during the next half-century the
Counter-Reformation regained much of the lost prestige and
influence of the Papacy, and drove back the advancing tide of
Protestantism. Despite the admitted importance of the reforms
effected in the Roman Church and the zeal of its champions, the
Society of Jesus, much of the responsibility for this reversal of
fortune must be ascribed to the divisions within the reformed
churches themselves. Nor did they show such ability to read the
signs of the times as to enable them to close their ranks and heal
their theological differences in face of the pressure of their
antagonist. From the advantage of taking the offensive against
a corrupt church which they had enjoyed during the first half of
the sixteenth century, they were driven into the disadvantageous
position of defending their conquests against a restored Papacy.
The strange contrast between the early victories and promise of
the reformed churches and the vigorous and successful counter-
reformation of the Church of Rome has led to exaggerated
depreciation of the results of the reformation movements. In
reaction against their pristine claims there has developed a
popular tendency to ignore the situation which provoked their
protest and to belittle the actual achievement of their separation.
Nor have they escaped the parallel tendency to saddle them with
the responsibility for various subsequent developments in European history in politics and economics which have been themselves the subject of criticism and disfavour. It is necessary to
essay some appreciation therefore of the results of the religious

changes of the sixteenth century alike upon the reformed churches and the Church of Rome, both in their internal administration and in their influence upon the world without.

In the sphere of religion, from which the Reformation movements sprang and with which they continued primarily concerned, two achievements of profound importance stand immediately to the credit of the reformed churches. The provision of forms of public worship in the vulgar tongue, and the installation of the vernacular throughout the divine service of their congregations were of inestimable advantage to the development of spiritual religion. The root principle of the liturgical experiments of all the reformed churches was that their service should be in a language understood of the people, and furthermore that it should be said in a completely audible voice by the minister in order that the congregation should follow the sequence of worship. In the several liturgies adopted by the reformed churches this principle found universal acceptance. Henceforth within their communion, the worship of God was to be in fact and truth *public* worship. Familiarity with this essential feature has obscured its revolutionary character in the sixteenth century and its permanent importance. The refusal of the Council of Trent to allow the Roman Mass to be said in the vernacular provides the best illustration of the achievement of the reformed churches in this vital field of worship. " I will pray with the spirit and I will pray with the understanding also; I will sing with the spirit and I will sing with the understanding also. Else if thou bless with the spirit, how shall he that filleth the place of the unlearned say the *Amen* at thy giving of thanks, seeing he knoweth not what thou sayest? For thou verily givest thanks well, but the other is not edified." Together with the vernacular Liturgy must be associated the congregational singing fostered by the German hymnody of the Lutheran churches and the *psaumes français* of the reformed. It can hardly be denied that this use of the vulgar tongue in divine service was one of the foremost influences upon popular religion developed by the reformed churches.

Associated with this principle so nearly as to be virtually inseparable was the provision of the whole Bible in the vernacular for the whole people. Partial translations from the Scriptures, especially of the Gospels and Psalms, had been published in the several countries of Western Europe towards the end of the fourteenth century; and the first German Bible was printed in 1466, whilst between that date and the publication of Luther's New Testament in 1522 no fewer than fourteen editions of the German Bible were printed, and four in Dutch. Most of these were used in religious houses, since orthodox opinion considered their free use by lay people dangerous, though episcopal licence was issued to well-born layfolk both in England and on the continent to use the vernacular Scriptures. The Reformers carried these limited precedents so much farther as to make their action almost a revolutionary innovation. They provided translations from the Hebrew and Greek originals instead of from the Latin Vulgate, their translations were unglossed, a feature unwarranted by traditional usage, and their vernacular Bibles were designed for all the people, not excluding the lowest classes of society, instead of only for the more prosperous. The results of this gift of the whole Bible to the whole people were of incalculable importance. Emphasis has been laid already upon the influence of the Bible upon the Anglican Ordinal. The ministry of the Word assumed a different character in consequence of the vernacular Bible. The Reformers' ideal of a weekly Eucharist on each Lord's Day, at which the people should attend both to hear sound doctrine preached from the pulpit and to receive the Holy Communion according to primitive custom, was frustrated by the conservatism of the laity. But the people gathered readily to hear sermons, expounding the hidden meaning of passages in the Scriptures which to the inexpert layman were dark and difficult of understanding. Nor, whilst regretting the failure of the Reformers to turn the Mass into a weekly Communion, should the benefits of the abolition of private Masses and of the cult of images and relics, with the corruptions and abuses associated in the popular mind with them in the fifteenth century, be forgotten.

More difficult to describe, because more intangible and private in nature, are the effects of the vernacular Bible upon the standards of domestic and individual piety. It is undoubted that the free and unrestricted perusal of the whole Bible privately at home as well as publicly in church evoked a new emphasis and character in popular religion. The head of the household, who had been enjoined in the fourteenth century to teach his family the Ave Maria, the Pater Noster, and the Apostles' Creed in the vulgar tongue, found a much wider field of instruction open to his efforts; and the practice of reading and explaining the Scriptures within the privacy of the family constituted a marked element in popular devotion. In public life the most recent historian of the early seventeenth century in England has testified that " at that time Englishmen studied the Bible with an intensity probably never equalled, and it is hardly possible to read a speech or writing of any length without perceiving its indebtedness to the Authorised Version ". Not in England only did the vernacular Bible furnish several generations of Christian laity with ' an outline of knowledge for boys and girls and their parents '.

In the spheres of public worship and individual religion, the reformed churches achieved changes of indubitable benefit. Less fortunate was the general tendency to exalt the Bible alone as the basis of doctrine. In protest against the parity of Scripture and unwritten tradition, the elevation of the former to a position of isolated authority was natural. Notwithstanding, its consequences were serious and soon evident. The generality of the Reformers were convinced of the inerrancy and absolute authority of the Bible and of the possibility of extracting from it a system of sound doctrine which would be final, and deniers of which would merit execution. They contended for a system of true belief against the false belief of the Roman Church, and not for the liberty of each individual to frame his own creed and confession of faith. Yet the ineluctable evidence of facts demonstrated the possibility of equally zealous and earnest Reformers (without the aid of the traditions of the Church) deducing very divergent doctrines from this one source. Herein lay the real importance, and the extreme unpopularity, of the Anabaptists of the sixteenth century. Far more grievous than the differences about Sacraments which divided Luther from Zwingli and Calvin were the doubts cast upon the doctrine of the Trinity in Unity from those advanced circles generally

associated with the Anabaptist movement. The offence of
Servetus was his denial of Trinitarian theology, for which he
suffered death at Geneva, as Gentile did at Berne. The execution
of individuals could not prevent the spread of their opinions,
and in 1551 the anti-Trinitarian tendencies began a notable
extension with the flight of the Italian Socinus to Poland. In the
immediate political and ecclesiastical situation these dissensions
amongst Protestants, which touched the very heart of the
Catholic faith, were of great disservice to the cause of the
Reformation and of equal service to that of the Counter-
Reformation.

More serious, however, than the contemporary effects of
disagreement was the problem created by the practical evidence
that ' the Bible and the Bible only as the religion of Protestants '
was productive of confusion, not unity, in belief. The use by
Calvin and even Zwingli of the weapon of death to quell heretics
could not dispose of the challenge of heresy. Nor could the
orthodox Reformers allow that anti-Trinitarian opinions ought
to be tolerated as a permissible variation of Protestantism. The
tendency, however, did not disappear with the lapse of time;
for the reformed churches were presented with such recurrent
spectacles as the decline of the great majority of Presbyterian
congregations in England during the eighteenth century into
Unitarianism. The Trinitarian controversies illustrated in fact
with penetrating clarity the unsoundness of the attempt to regard
the Bible alone as the basis of doctrine. For apart from the
history of patristic theology the orthodox doctrine of the
Trinity can hardly be extracted from the New Testament. Moreover the lack of understanding of historical development in the
formulation of Christian theology was a hindrance to the
refutation in argument of heterodox opinions. The antipathy
to tradition was not a passing phase, but rather increased
until during the eighteenth century a widespread movement of
rationalistic criticism of creeds and Scriptures tended to under-
mine the foundations of Christine doctrine.

Unfortunately the Roman Church could afford no useful
assistance in such crises. For, although its reliance upon tradition
enabled it to maintain its dogmatic position, its insistence upon

the parity of Scripture and unwritten tradition tempted it to add to the œcumenical definitions of Christian faith, new articles entirely unfounded upon any Biblical evidence whatever, as was seen in the definition by Pius IX in 1854 of the dogma of the Immaculate Conception of the Blessed Virgin Mary. There was evident need of a *via media* between the rigid exclusion of tradition on the one hand and the assertion of its equal authority with the Bible on the other. In the Anglican definition of the Church as the witness and keeper of Holy Writ, but unable to define anything to be believed of necessity for eternal salvation which could not be proved therefrom, there was the possibility of such a mediating position. In the *Laws of Ecclesiastical Policy* of Richard Hooker, his defence of the Anglican position was based upon the triple grounds of Scripture, Tradition, and Reason. The province of Reason was strictly limited in six-teenth-century debate by the general belief in the inerrancy of the Bible, so that what was evidently prescribed by Holy Scrip-ture was not subject to criticism. Three centuries later, however, when the nineteenth century witnessed the rise of the move-ment of literary and historical criticism of the Bible itself, reason ascended to a new position of importance in Christian apologetic. The reformed churches were driven to admission of the pres-ence of error in the Scriptures, and therewith to a more generous acknowledgment of the place of tradition and reason in the definition of doctrine. Thus the disproportion of the sixteenth-century reformed theology was redressed; and by judicious acceptance of the claims of tradition and reason, theologians of the reformed churches were able to assimilate the new know-ledge and to preserve the proportion of the Faith.

The Church of Rome developed in the contrary direction. The contest between Papacy and episcopate which had been left in suspense at Trent, was determined at the Vatican Council of 1870 by the definition of papal infallibility. The conciliar decree recognised the character of infallibility in *ex cathedra* papal utter-ances upon faith and morals, in virtue of the authority of the Papacy itself, not of the assent of the Church. (Romani pontificis definitiones ex sese non autem ex consensu ecclesiae irreforma-biles esse.) Moreover, to the challenge of the movement of

Biblical criticism, Rome replied by a reaffirmation of the complete inerrancy of the whole Bible, and of the traditional authorship of its several books, and by an anti-Modernist oath to exclude dissentients from its communion. Little room for doubt remains that in meeting the crisis of Biblical criticism the advantage lay with the churches of the reformed tradition.

Although the Reformers of the sixteenth century were not the parents of religious toleration, the many divisions of their churches led in the course of history to their acceptance of the principle of toleration by the state of differences of religious creed and profession. The continuing weakness of the reformed churches, however, has lain in their lack of cohesion. Even if the principle of uniformity was driven to extremes in the post-Tridentine Church of Rome, the fissiparous character of the reformed churches made them liable to such satire as that levelled in Bossuet's *Histoire des Variations des Églises Protestantes*, and to the practical disadvantages of inability to co-operate. The increasing indifference, if not hostility, of many twentieth-century States to Christianity has led the reformed churches of Europe to explore possibilities of common action, and to the creation of an œcumenical movement which stretches beyond the nations of the Old World. Progress in such an enterprise involves reconsideration of the considerable divergencies of the reformed churches in both faith and order, for the widespread abandonment of episcopacy in the sixteenth century constitutes a barrier to unity. Despite such movements towards unity, the historical circumstances of the Reformation epoch, which drove the reformed churches into positions of varying antagonism to Rome and the Roman Church into a situation of unyielding rigidity, have produced unfortunate consequences in weakening the influence and authority of Christianity in the modern world.

But, if the reformed churches have contributed much to the development of personal religion and to the reconciliation of Christianity with human knowledge and discovery, the Reformation movements have been charged with responsibility for some developments in European society towards which they can hardly be thought to stand in the relation of effective cause. Thus they have been charged with responsibility for the growth of nationalism and the omnicompetent modern State. In fact nationalism had grown to maturity during the later Middle Ages, within the papal obedience and despite the theory of a single Christian State presided over by pope and emperor. The Reformation movements were indeed powerfully influenced by the national kingdoms, and saw in the Christian prince the only practical alternative to the oppressive and corrupt Italian Papacy. Nationalism developed independently of Protestantism, and it would be difficult to discover a more determinedly national kingdom than the France of Louis XIV, despite the fact that this king withdrew the toleration accorded by his predecessors to the Huguenots and thereby testified his zeal for Roman Catholicism. The difficulties which the Papacy met in its diplomatic relations with the several European States owning its spiritual allegiance are sufficient evidence of the fact that nationalism was not a product of Protestant and reformed kingdoms alone. Nor can the Papacy itself escape the verdict of history on its political situation and its close identification with Italian secular politics, which resulted in the see of Peter becoming the close preserve of Italian ecclesiastics. The political and international problems associated with the rise of national States were the results of the Middle Ages rather than of the Reformation movements.

More remote from historical fact is the interpretation which sees in the Reformation nothing other than a religious cloak for economic change. Undoubtedly civil princes and the nobles and merchants of their domains looked with covetous avarice upon the rich estates of bishoprics, cathedrals, and monastic foundations, and hastened to turn religious reformation to commercial profit. But it is difficult to carry this admitted connection so far as to see in the religious revolution only the reflection of economic changes. Nor should it be forgotten that in countries untouched by any large measure of Protestant doctrines, similar economic changes to those experienced in sixteenth-century England, Germany and Sweden ensued in later epochs, as in the French Revolution at the end of the eighteenth century, in the nineteenth-century Italy, and in contemporary Spain. Similarly the attempt to explain Calvinism by its particular business morality and emphasis upon the importance of secular professions as a divine vocation and to deduce therefrom the development of the capitalist system is not to be accepted without large reserve. It is indisputable that the large capitalist business houses of the fifteenth century had their centres in Catholic lands and were presided over by Catholics; and manifestly they had sprung up under the ægis of the Church if not with its patronage. In this, as in other aspects, the close of the Middle Ages was a period of change and transition; and the Reformation movements were an element in such change.

Fundamentally therefore the Reformation must be judged to be a series of movements for religious change and must be judged as such. Of the imperative need for reform the Counter-Reformation itself provided sufficient testimony; nor must it be forgotten that the post-Tridentine Roman Church was a very different institution from its corrupt predecessor which provoked the actual outbreak of revolt. It is impossible to forecast what would have been the fortunes of Christianity if the Reformers had been faced by a reformed Papacy, such as resulted from the Council of Trent. In the financial, judicial, and administrative spheres the presence of abuses and the necessity of reform is universally admitted.

In the more specifically religious field it can hardly be doubted that the Reformation registered a considerable advance towards the ideal of spiritual and personal religion, despite its manifest imperfections. These imperfections are strikingly evident; for the Protestant theologies were often as rigid and narrow as those from which the Reformers had reacted, and the violent break with tradition resulted in loss, such as the widespread abandonment of episcopacy and the rejection of the monastic vocation. Nor can the historian of Christianity register any other sentiment than profound regret at the spectacle of rival churches, Roman and reformed, in conscious opposition and reaction to each other, exaggerating and carrying to extremes principles which in many respects were complementary rather than contradictory. Notwithstanding, the reformed Confessions of Faith were not incapable of modification, since no character of formal infallibility attached to them. In principle, moreover, the reformed churches opened the way, even if their first representatives did not tread far upon it, to a more critical, scholarly, and veracious treatment of the Biblical, historical, theological, and liturgical elements in the Christian tradition; for it is essential to the genius of Christianity to bring out of its treasure store things new and old. Most particularly by their adoption of the vulgar tongue in public worship and by their provision of the whole Bible in the vernacular to the whole people, the reformed churches looked towards the fulfilment of that New Covenant, of which the Christian Church is the servant in its ministry alike of the Word and Sacraments, and whereof it was written:

This is the covenant that I will make with the house of Israel after those days, saith the Lord: I will put my law in their inward parts, and in their heart will I write it; and I will be their God and they shall be my people; and they shall teach no more every man his neighbour and every man his brother, saying, Know the Lord: for they shall all know me, from the least of them unto the greatest, saith the Lord.